FOG AT THE MANASSAS BATTLEFIELD

FOG AT THE MANASSAS BATTLEFIELD

Poems by
Patrick Bizzaro

Photography by
Resa Crane Bizzaro

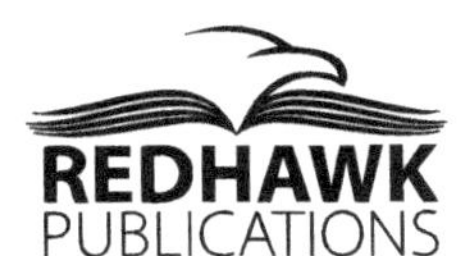

Fog At The Manassas Battlefield

Redhawk Publications
The Catawba Valley Community College Press
2550 US Hwy 70 SE
Hickory NC 28602

ISBN: 978-1-959346-01-2

Library of Congress Control Number: 20229522023

Poems: Patrick Bizzaro
Photography: Resa Crane Bizzaro
Cover Design & Layout: Jamie Bruckmann
Cover Image: Resa Crane Bizzaro

This book was not laid out by Redhawk Publications and the blank pages are intentional. No content has been lost or left out.

redhawkpublications.com

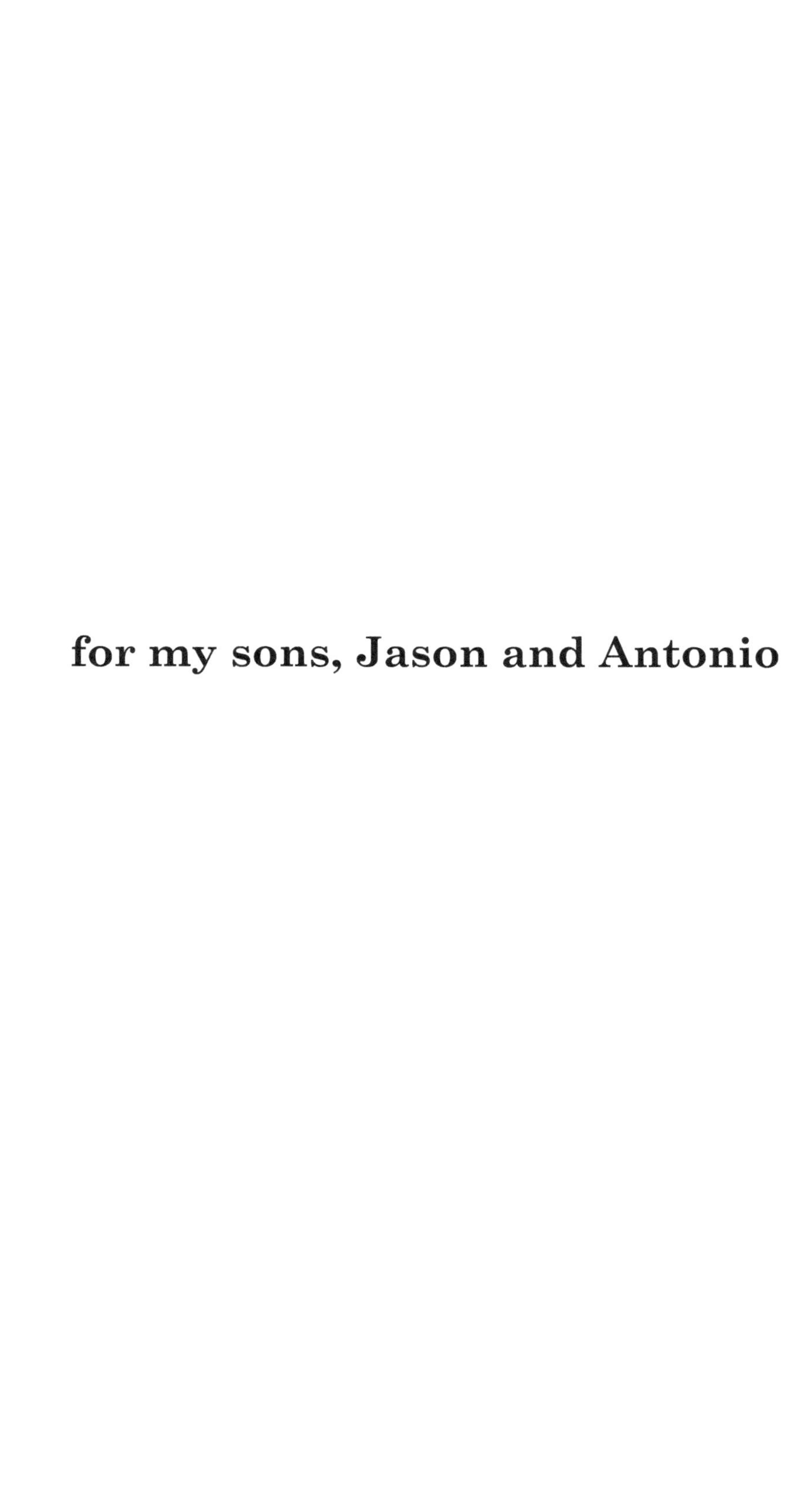

for my sons, Jason and Antonio

TABLE OF CONTENTS

Part III: In Hostile Climates 59

Part IV: Violence 91

AUTHOR'S INTRODUCTION

In some ways this volume is my collected poems if "collected" poems are a product not of the poet's age and health but of the age of the poems in the book. Among the poems that appear in this book, for instance, "Manassas" is the oldest, written nearly fifty years ago, shortly after I took a teaching job at Northern Virginia Community College in Manassas, a campus adjacent to the Manassas Battlefield Park. "Manassas" won the *Four Quarters* Poetry Prize from LaSalle University in 1978. I remarked then, formally and informally, on what I have repeated often over the past half century, my belief that poetry has potential to stand for a great many things in our culture, including our evolving understandings of the world. And maybe it does.

A central theme in the volume, expressed in a poem written during that same early period in my life as a writer, "Violence," may be a case in point. "Violence" was published first as a poetry pamphlet by Tamarack Editions in 1979 and was soon thereafter, according to my editor, the late Alley Hoey, adopted as a textbook for a graduate course in sociology at Syracuse University. That insight about poetry-as-a-way-of-knowing was suggested to me by an unnamed sociologist who found a way to make the subject of human violence presentable by using a poem. That act encouraged me to continue to contemplate ways in which poetry could tell certain truths different in their expression from the accumulation of "facts" we are apt to find in a sociology textbook, which is likely to offer a reasoned explanation of everything from angry outbursts to declarations of war.

In the Post-truth era in which we live, no one can be certain that the most effective model of thinking we have traditionally employed in reaching conclusions is more rhetorical than poetic, more "reasoned" than "imagined." Clearly, traditional evidence is under attack. This fact has ramifications we are only now beginning to feel in our daily lives. For instance, are our insights into what constitutes truth and, therefore, what should be passed forward to our children a product of syllogism or, more nuanced, of "a timely utterance [that] gave that thought relief," to bring Wordsworth into this argument, logic or creative imagining? That thought occurred to me long ago, but I have continued to contemplate it, especially in my recollection of places where I have lived and written about and how my perception of those places affected who I have become.

It is no surprise that "Violence" begins in uncertainty, "A man never knows/what will happen/ if someone places a gun/in his hands." But what this poem does is state the predicament that serves as the foundation for this collection of poems: Are wars inside us (as anger or hate or resentment) before we engage in them with (that is, take them out on) others?

My relationship with the Manassas Battlefield was quite personal, beginning in thought and then transitioning into action. On a typical workday in the mid-1970s, I would finish teaching, change into my running gear and jog by myself through the bridle trails that traverse the park.

My feeling of propriety surprised me, so on weekends I'd share "my park" with my son, Jason, barely more than an infant at the time, on what he and I called our walk-runs. Always articulate and insightful, Jason asked a lot of questions. To answer them, I often had to consult various books on the subject, some of them cited in this volume. The insights in those books, a proper complication arising from a young child's questionings, constitute the beginnings of several other historical poems important to my imaginings here. Thank you, young Jason!

When I left Manassas to take a job at East Carolina University, my love of the Battlefield stayed with me, and I continued writing these poems, obsessively at times. I returned often to Manassas to run on those trails, and I continued to read history books about the battles there. Some of the poems I wrote during my first several years at ECU appeared in limited edition chapbooks published by Mount Olive College Press. But those poems had not been collected until now and made to appear together as one volume.

While "Manassas" was the first poem in this collection to be written, the most recent of them was "Building a House of History," written in 2022. In it and in several other poems, the rhetorician in me asked hard questions about what constitutes history. It interests me as a poet and as a student of history that history tells a narrative but that that story gets changed and reinterpreted and then reinterpreted again, as it should. After all, reinterpretation is a human act of control over who we think we are and what human actions mean to us, even as some influencers change and others emerge. As I say in that poem, "the structures we live by/differ at the brick foundation ... so people we have never seen/can enter/and make it a house of their own."

So, it is not surprising that, as a nurturing father to my children (Jason, Krissy and Antonio), the knowledge I gained by inhabiting the woods the way I did as a young, untenured professor proved to be quite useful. Articulating those insights is something I joyfully share with them in the making of this volume. What's more, much as I share my life with my talented wife, Dr. Resa Crane Bizzaro, the well-known scholar of Indigenous rhetorics, I gladly share this part of my life's work on which she has made her mark with her wonderfully appropriate photos.

This is our book, and I am honored to share this space with you, dear reader.

Patrick Bizzaro
Indiana, PA
December 9, 2022

PART I: BUILDING A HOUSE OF HISTORY

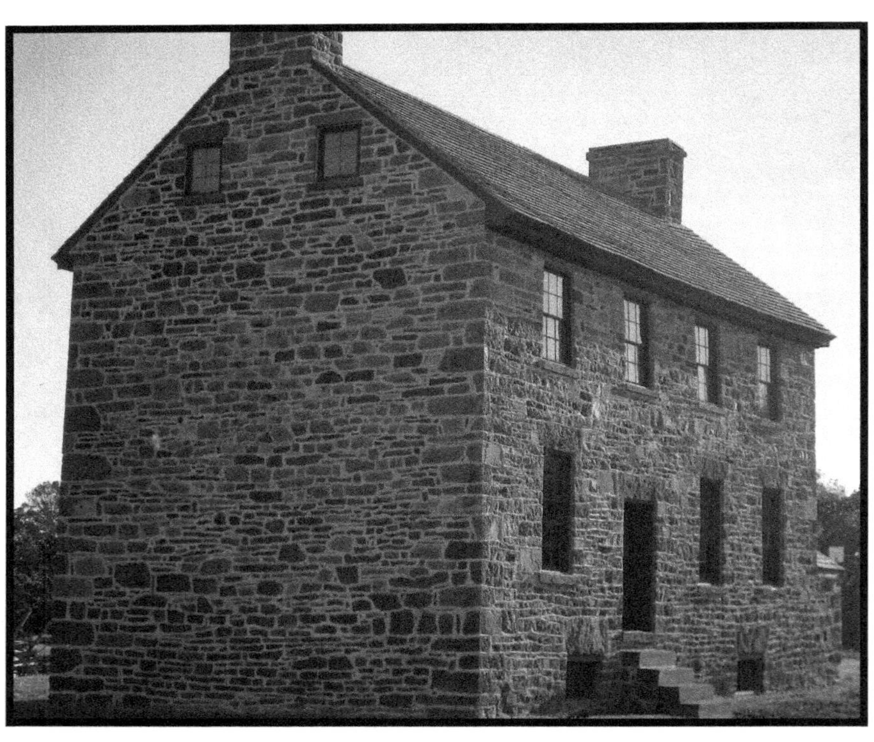

BUILDING A HOUSE OF HISTORY

for Wendy Bishop

In the lot
across the street, four men enter
my vision, all doing almost
what I think they're doing,

all building a house
cooperating with the movement of dirt
to a designated spot across the yard,
all building one house
from a single plan.

But as I watch, I see
ahead of their weary motions
the house of my understanding
and the house of theirs
though all the while
they ignore me

as if the structures we live by
differ at the brick foundation,
and the house this will become
is finished as they begin it,
stretched to its imaginary
boundaries, so people
we have never seen
can enter
and make it a house of their own.

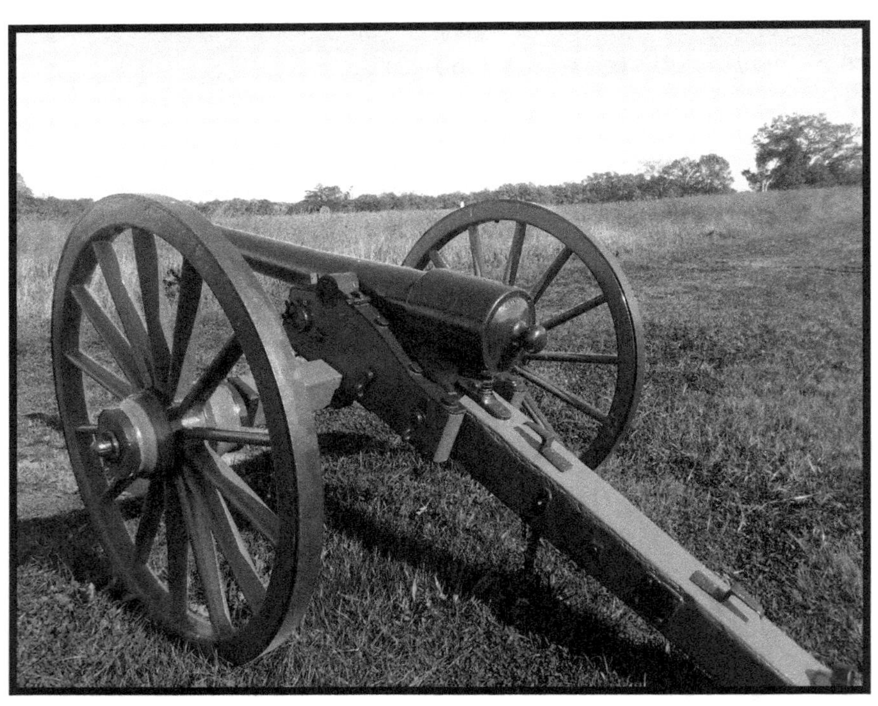

INTERRUPTIONS

Interruptions suspend the continuous accumulation of knowledge, interrupt its slow development, and force it to enter a new time.

Foucault, The Archeology of Knowledge

History is the history of spaces,
interruptions, gaps.
A cause does not dictate
an effect, as we long thought.

If I dig a hole over there and find
a Civil War musket, and you dig a hole
alongside it and find a bullet, we cannot conclude
the bullet was shot from the musket.
We are mistaken to believe
someone, some Civil War soldier,
must have held the rifle.

There are interruptions all around us,
and they do not connect to "silent
beginnings" or continuous futures.

Even archeologists know
we can never get closer than half-way.
The true order of things
is the sequence of interruptions.
That's all we know for sure
and all we need to know
for now.

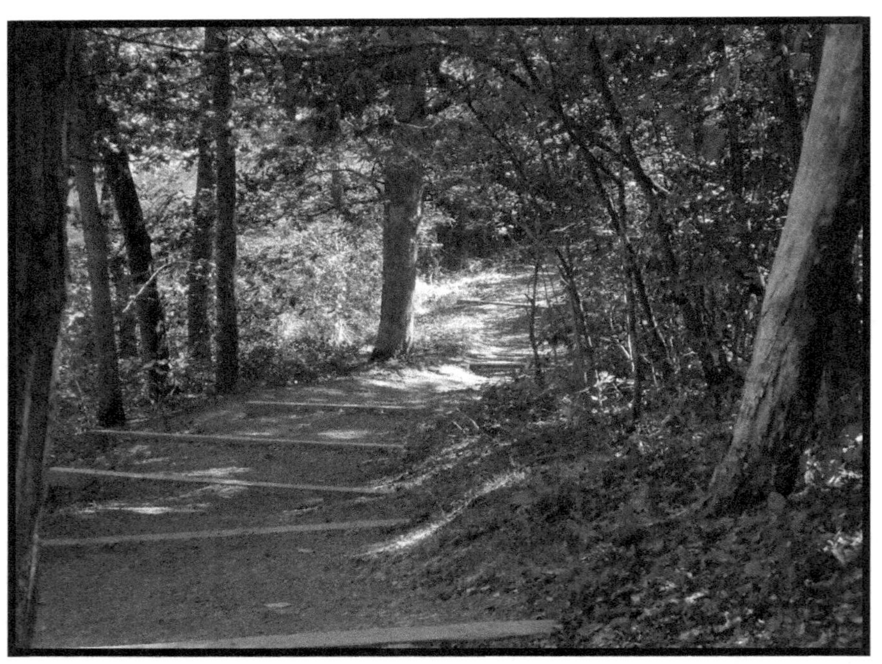

REMINDER

for Resa

Running down the Battlefield's
rocky trails, I raise one flat palm
as a reminder
that I am surrounded,
as a plea for forgiveness
for boldly entering the Manassas Battlefield
alone, at night.

My hand guides me
through the dark.
But if it were day,
I'd still travel cautiously,
hand in this position,
as though ahead of me
just beyond my reach
is a door
I must push open carefully
so as not to stumble through
the glass.

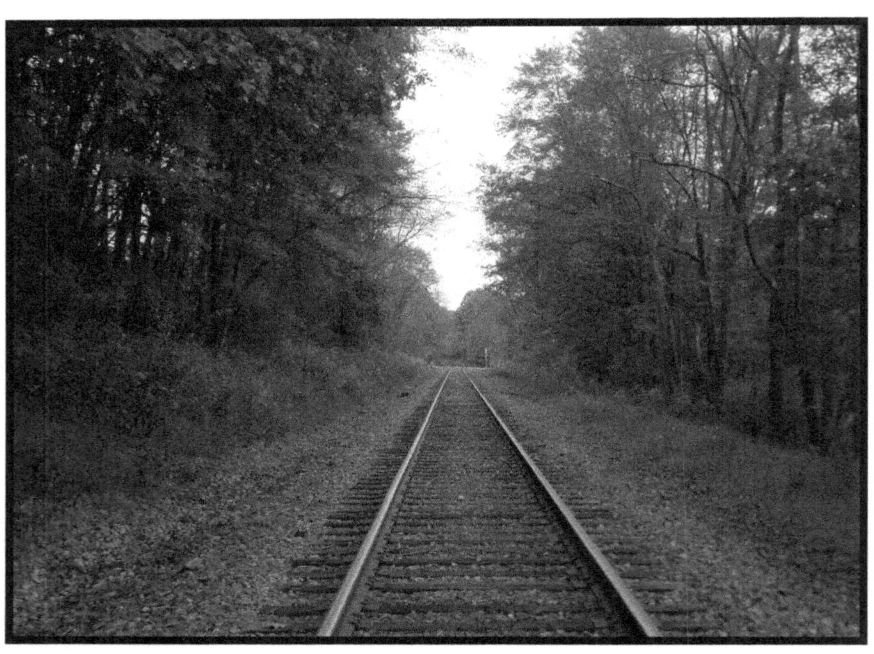

MANASSAS STATION

Soldiers who died here knew
crosses of wheat bordering train tracks,
oil of fear on hands and eyes,
odor of death on passing wheels.

A train through Manassas meant
a station busy as smoke,
old men standing alone waving,
enduring the crusts of their skin,

old women fat with tears
watching someone's son
shake an empty sleeve
as he passed.

Last night, I walked to the station
where it stands beside Brady's
Bar. Boards shivered
as I climbed steps

toward windows shuttered
with wood from old benches, made during
forgotten wars. I lit a cigarette,
made circles in the dark.

Far off, a light circled above the tracks,
then the station shivered.
A train passed, and I waved.
But only boxcars bounced by,

only flatbeds of yellow tractors,
only a circus of Fords.
Afterwards, I walked
to the middle of the tracks

and squatted on a rail until early summer
lightning opened the skies
and I felt someone
creeping up behind me.

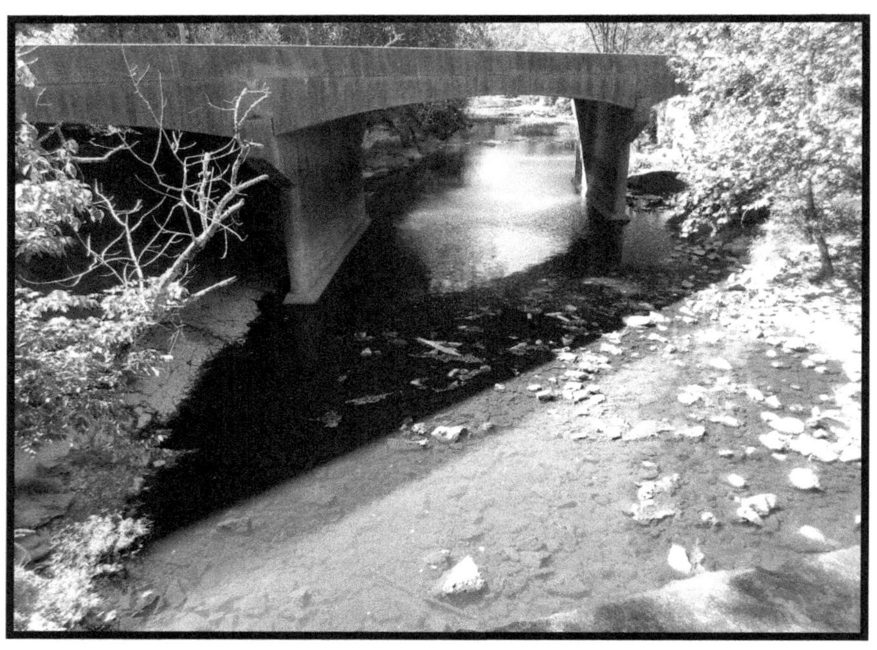

VIRGINIA SPRING

It starts white as your whisper.
Cow bones lean against
splintered barns
where snow first recedes.
Prints of bird claws
deepen in the snow
until they grow
spider webs in the mud.

In the distance, a boy
takes his father's hand
and walks in the shallow river
pausing among trees.
The boy notices wet weeds
closing around his knees
and debris carried miles
by the slow current.

He knows spring
in the eyes of his father
and in the odor of fish
among tall weeds.
He looks down,
into the brown stream
and finds for the first time
his own shiny reflection.

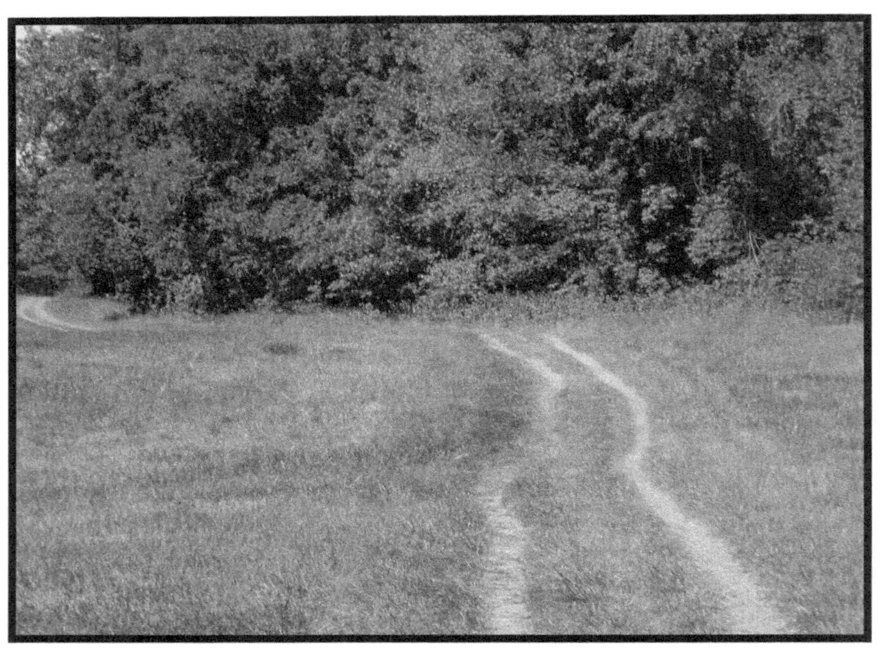

TOBACCO FIELDS

Each year we wonder
how Bull Run survives
the heat, how sun
along its banks
passes slim as water
snakes through branches
to startle life
despite forgotten rain,
unfolded grass.

This is tobacco season
and we are long drawn and thin
this year as last,
recalling lines
of tobacco,
hunched and silent.

This is tobacco season
and we dream of narrow
paths through rows and rows,
recalling children who discovered
in these fields
their own shiny reflections,
their own slim dreams
of futures that wave
out in front of them
in the sunshine,
in the Virginia heat.

And we recall harvest
come at last
so thick we smell it
in this late summer perfume,
so rich we know its presence
in our children's eyes,
in their smiles,
tobacco juice running
when they speak,
smelling of earth,
of youth,
of this season
that has come without warning
into our fields,
into our lives.

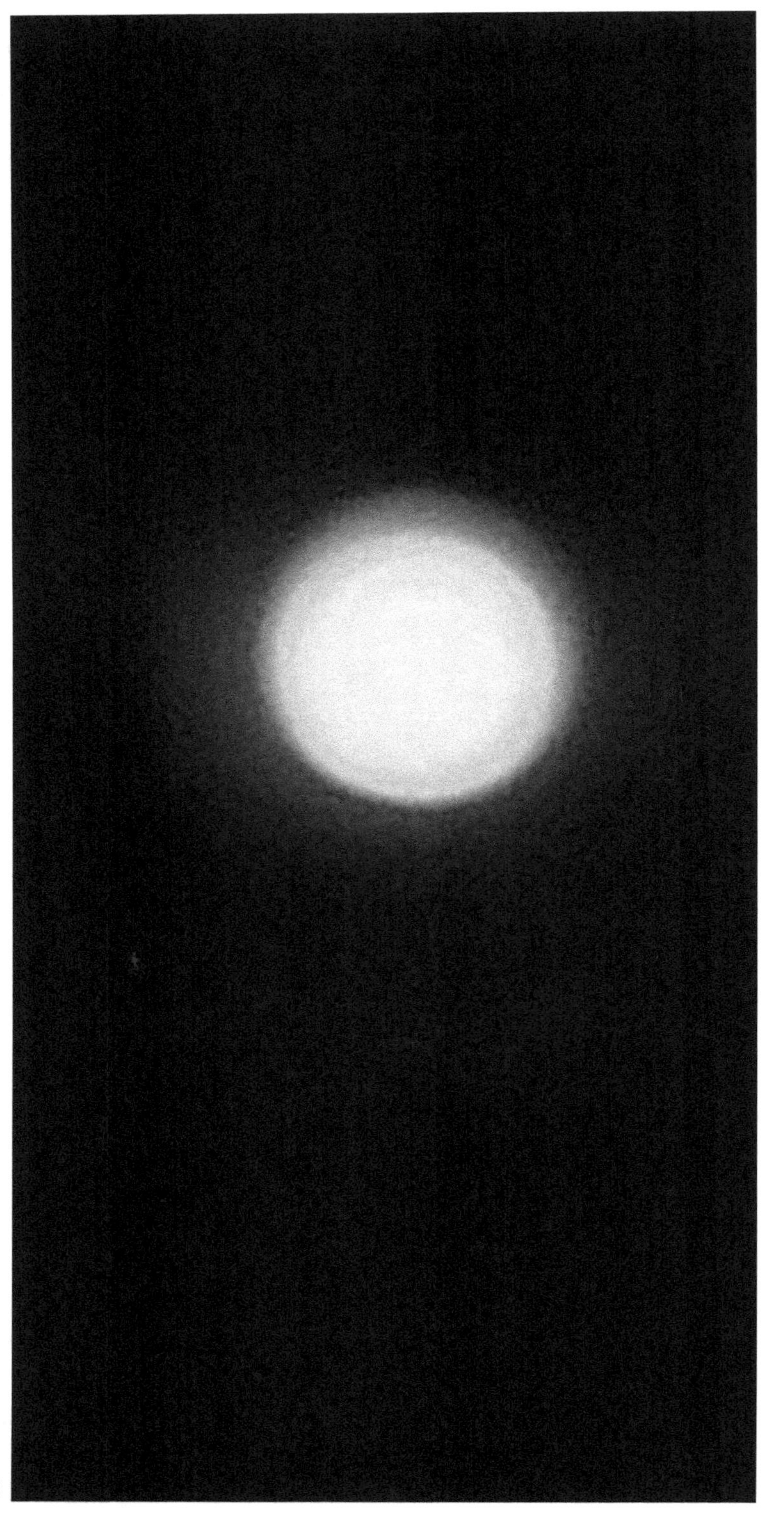

FOG AT THE MANASSAS BATTLEFIELD

for Jason

Pines rise above the fog
like pointed beaks of birds.
Far below, where I walk with my son,
fog might once have been smoke
where a man burned
through the echoes of war.

At this thought-turned-word
we stop, my son and I,
to watch what forms against the air,
what rises from our shallow lips
like breaths of dying men and boys
young as mine
whose faces shimmered through the trees.

When we lean against a stump,
I move an ear closer to my son
until his warm breath turns fog against
my cheek. His white whisper
tells me *listen*:

all around us
old trees ache with wind,
birds crack through trees,
and the moon, cold and alone,
rolls through low branches
into bushes at our feet.

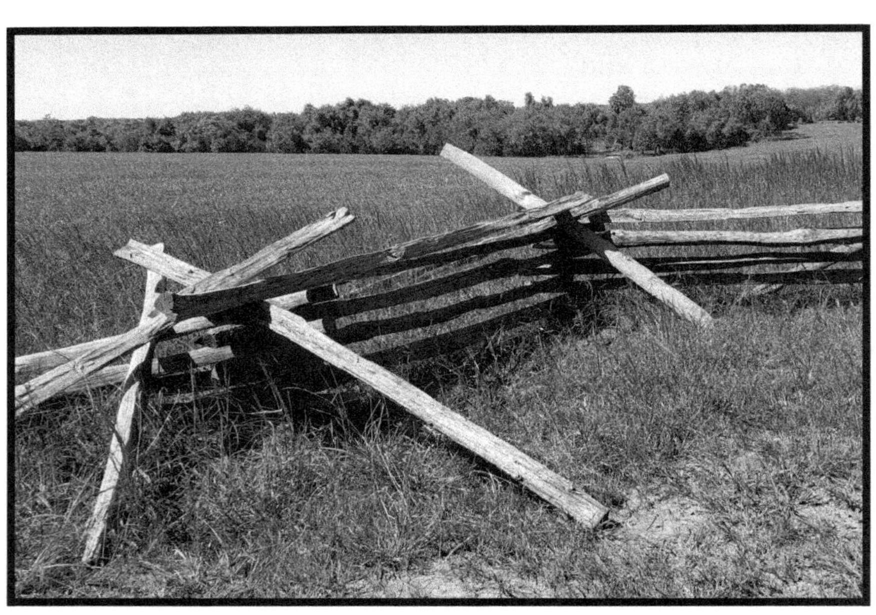

THE OTHER SIDE

for Maddie Vestal

They say that's where death is,
too near to avoid,
too far away to claim
as this side.

The other side disguises itself
as someplace else,
as far away as possible
but still part of the whole.

I have seen the other side
in the eyes of friends and enemies.
Like the pulley clothesline in your yard,
it can be pulled nearer

and pulled more
to be farther. Those of us
on this side know
the other side is simply us, reversed.

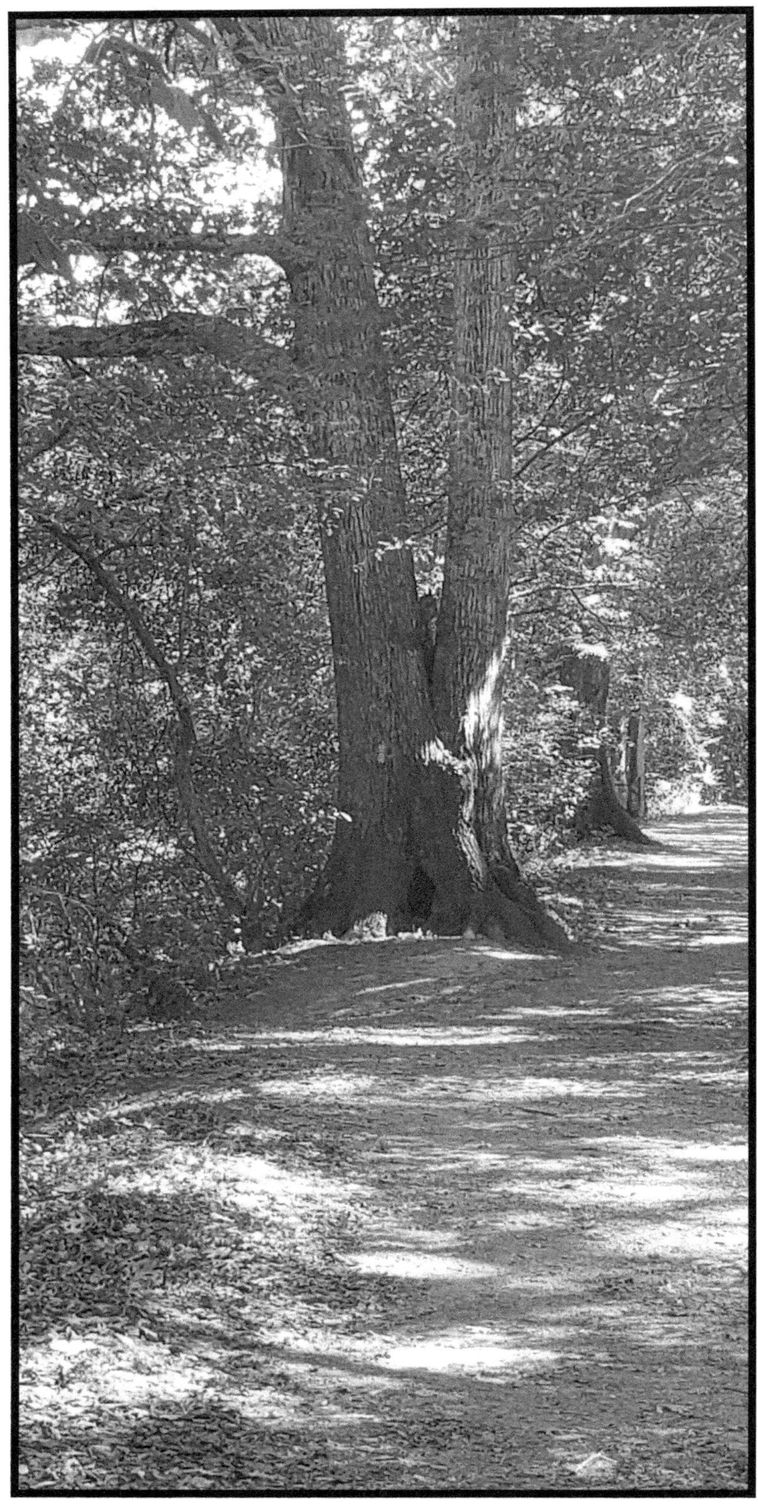

DARK HORIZON

The Gentler sex who disguised themselves and swapped brooms for muskets were able to sustain the deception for amazingly long periods of time.

Ben Wiley

One late afternoon, in a scientific
state of mind, I watched men enter
the Battlefield. At sunset,
they looked to the glowing horizon
until sun flattened all that remained of day.
They pointed at shining bellies of birds
coasting flyways and red-brown
chestnut clouds sinking
lightly into night.

Behind them
along the dark horizon, the outline of soldier-
women disguised as hilltops marching to war
stared at us, tears falling through the trees
like raindrops of blood,
becoming stones at the horizon,
then vanishing to resist future description.

These acts of deception are permanently recorded there
stories of women disguised as men
to serve as soldiers while men in the park
watched the sun disguised as a symbol of peace.

I remember my son
turning his head
to the darkening horizon.

From this distance, he imagined the Blue Ridge
to be filled with faces: broad soldier necks
growing from mountains
and women, hair once piled
atop their heads,
counting drops of blood
falling from soldier necks
into stones at the horizon.

In unity, some stories from the War
became the stories of beautiful
if unintentional suicides
told by women disguised as soldiers
who would watch sunset
after they thought they'd grabbed it,
swallowed it,
and would glow forever
from within.

But the men in the park at sunset
never turn their heads.
Whether they are soldiers of the sun
and must watch themselves sink
beneath the horizon
or butterflies with sun
falling through their
beautiful wings,
they don't turn around.
And if they do once
and watch dark
close in above them,
they will see women unified

to their men through a cause,
committing the stone suicides
my son and I could only see
off in the blurry distance
where we imagined women
who thought they'd found the sun.

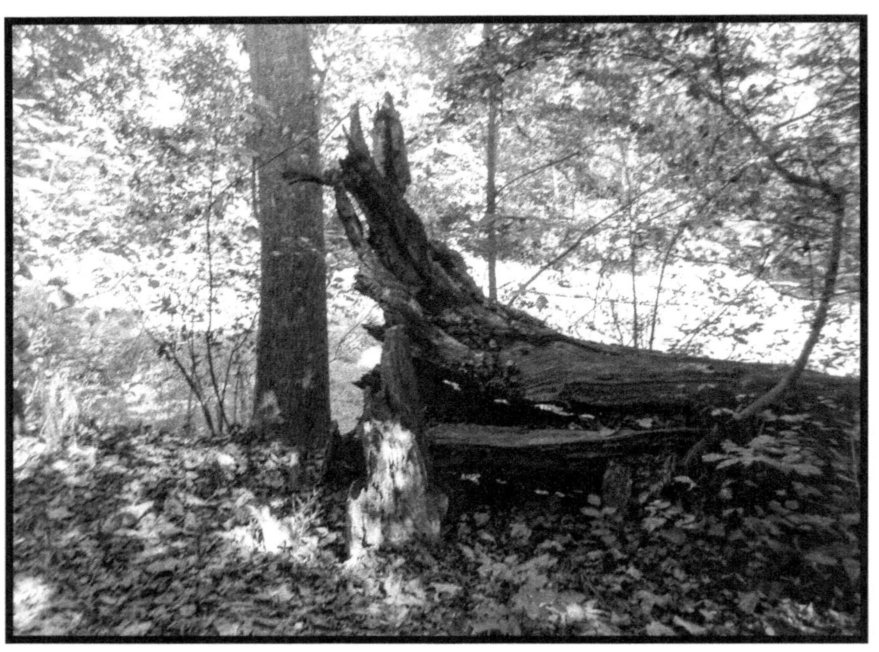

YOUR COLD DREAM

for my mother (b 1920, d 1985)

The time will come
when you'll ask why
we've worn
so little clothing
to greet the cold weather,
the icy winds of your dream.
And we'll stand before you,
shivering multitudes
who watch the plotting sky
for the answer.

One of us will step forward and say
this is, after all,
a dream, this is,
after all, a line-up of people
remembered.
Should we make special occasions
for simple thoughts?

We would have dressed better
had we known we would be called
to this cold dream,
to this recollection
that spells its life
with letters fingered
in our breaths.

We would have worn overcoats
for the great snows of recollection,
old overcoats with torn cuffs

and knit gloves pulled
onto the sleeves themselves so nothing,
not the cold air, not the snow
in our palms
might rub our skin
cold and red and fingertip hard.

We would have wrapped our great
triangular faces in scarves
and wrapped those scarves around our necks
and let one long end blow out in the wind
like a shout from cold lips,
laughing as it swung around
and struck us in the face.
We would have come with our tender arms
outspread, ready to enter this cold,
this snow at our feet,
this dream you have placed us in
here, in the blizzard,
so poorly dressed.

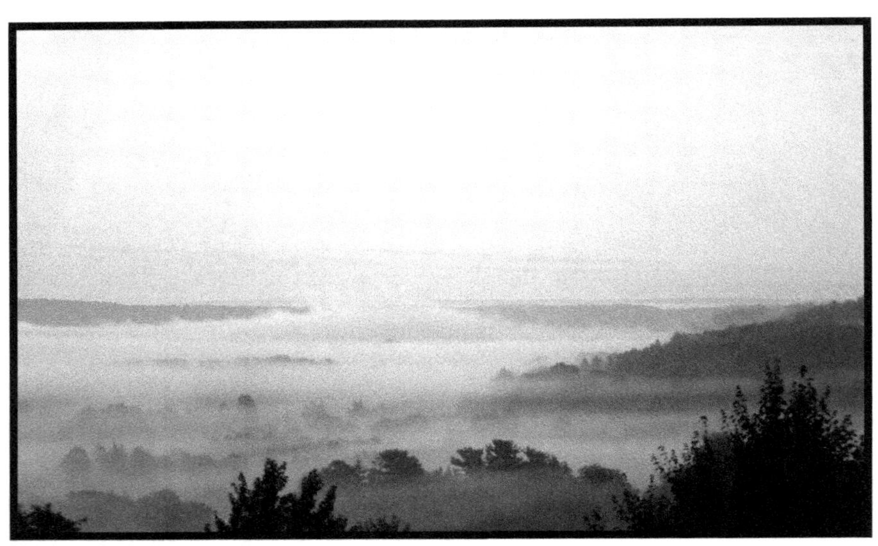

STILLNESS

I remember her as stillness
standing over the valley
searching for the edge
of the cliff's shadow.
It was night.

She must have been wishing
she could fly,
her arms spread
above stars that clung
to her sides. She was
a crow ready to wrench
shiny objects from
the night. Her song
drifted softly over
the valley, collapsing
flatly against cliff walls.

She was a darkness
falling from angles
seen only through
corners of the eyes,
a stillness
giving motion
to the night.

PART II: THE TASTE OF ROPE

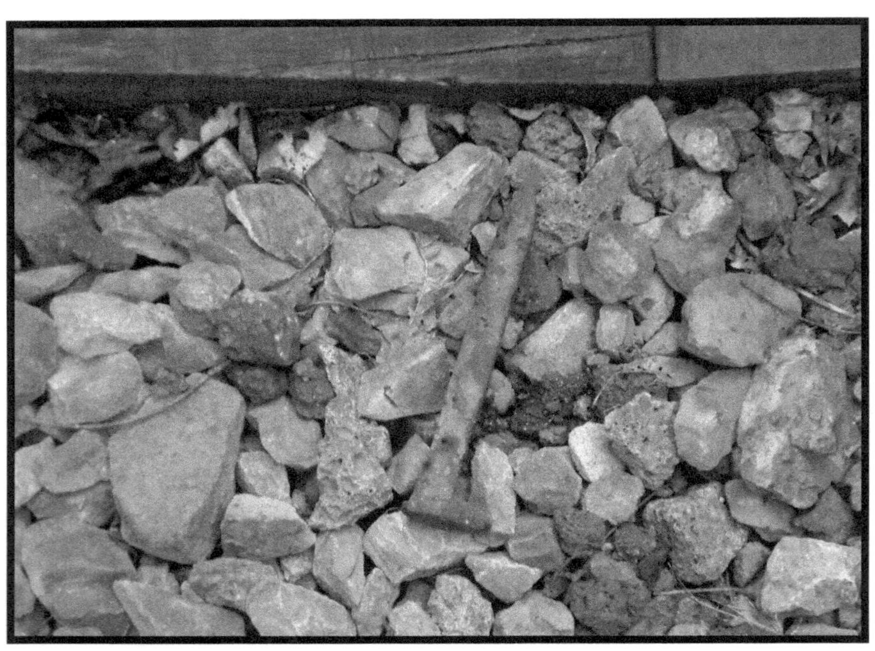

THE TASTE OF ROPE

1.

In my photo album
a boy in Civil War hat,
carrying a shotgun and flag
of stars and bars,
sits on a horse's
swaying back.

Furrows, where a plow horse
harness has worn maps,
tunnel the horse's sides.
Its wet flanks burst
against the boy's thighs.

Above his wide
brim, a cloud strains
against dry morning air.
Sun half shines.
Beneath his chest,
the horse's weathered nostrils.

2.

Driving through Fauquier
County, Virginia, I note
a horse head rock
decapitated from the mountain.
Its distant eyes:
deep-set, drizzly.
Its nostrils, soundless
and narrow.

From across the field
separating mountain from road,
I hear the tug of harness
on a plow horse, the grate
of ground beneath a plow.

The slow, glazed eye
of the plow horse
follows our car.
From the back seat,
my son shouts to me,
calling the nag pony.

I hope my son
will never know
the taste of rope.

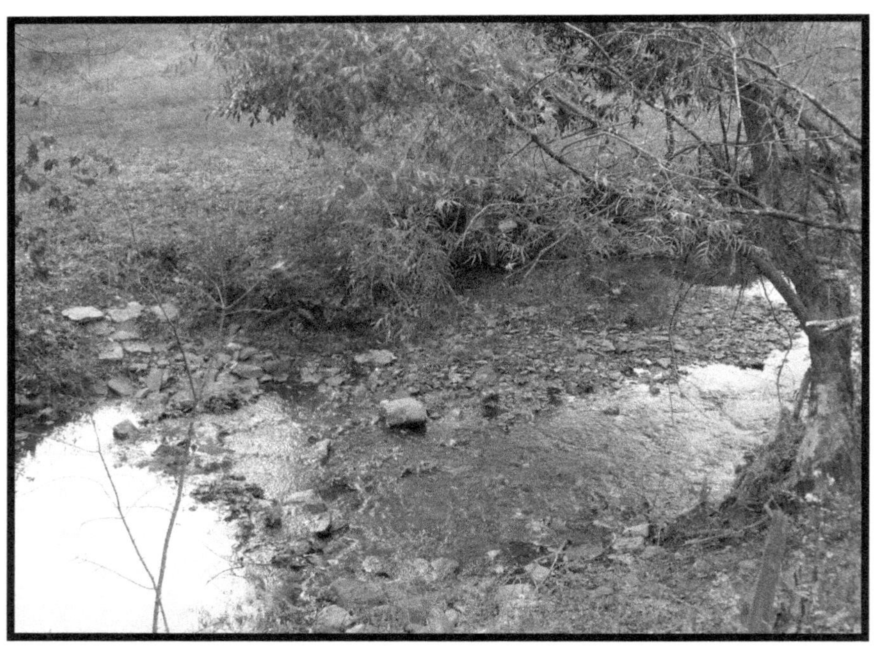

BOOTS

I awaken
from depths of Sabbath quiet.
Night blurs my eyes.

In the corner
muddy boots—open graves
of yesterday's travels.

Empty holes, they glow from the floor.
I roll to my side
taking them with me.

Beneath my slow, drowsy lids,
I retrace the path
I walked the night before.

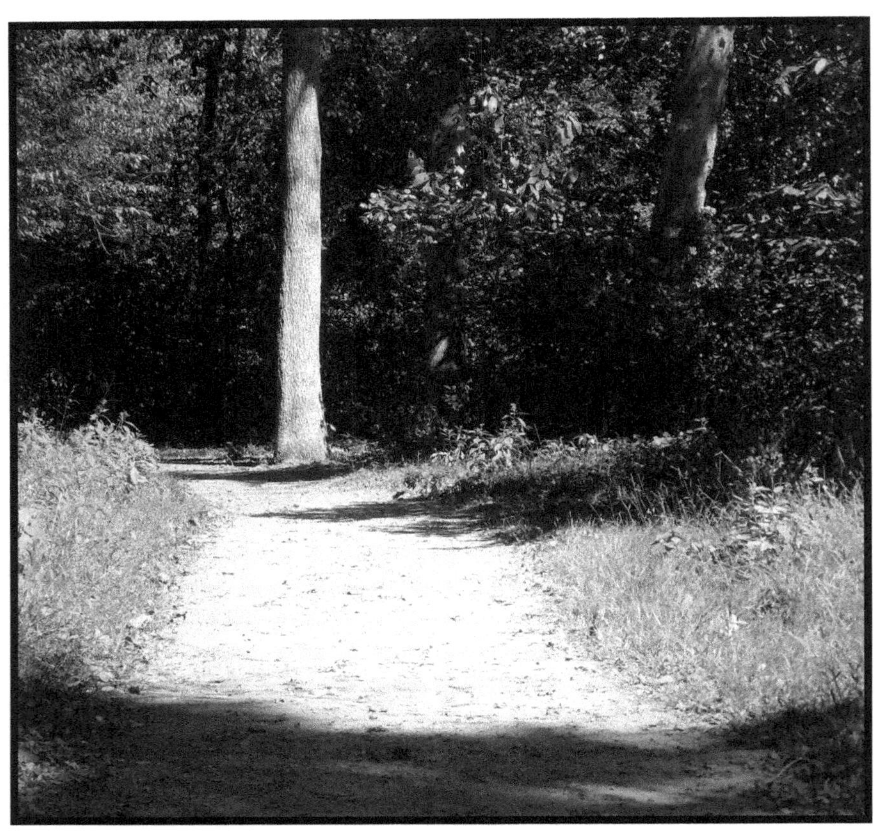

HANGING TREE

It forces remembrance
of something swinging through the night.
A tree limb following
the moon's slow arc,

a gate door
loose among tall weeds.
I remember the sound
of an empty hand exploding

silence and an audience
whose eyes form circles
against a background of setting sun
and Blue Ridge mountain.

Hives of passion
rise to my arms
as a horse jolts forward
beneath a lifeless branch of tree.

And the horse too remembers slow pain
against its rump
as the weight he carries
pulls backward,

pulled by the hanging tree
which has no pulse
though I have seen it shake
in my dreams from the weight

of something dressed for war
dying in its boots, something swinging,
hanging, moving its legs
as though to run.

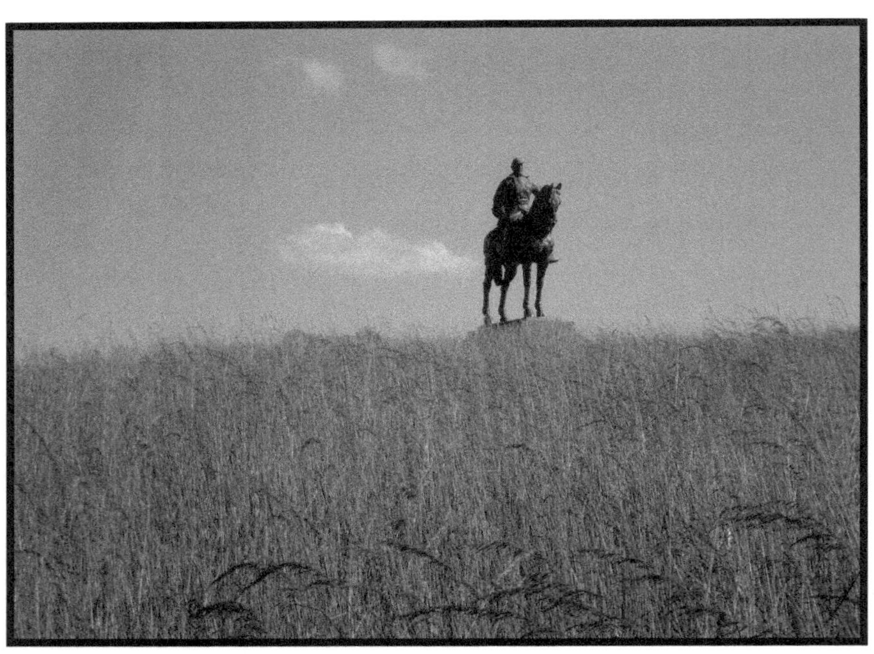

RUNNING AT THE MANASSAS BATTLEFIELD

Today my son runs with me,
his first day out. This is simple
ritual, not a bear hunt or a search
for claw marks in the mud.

This is just a run, our heads down,
my son in front of me, leaning beneath the tree
that rips patterns of limbs
across my ribs.

Moving downhill, twisting
from a branch, my foot latches anyway
beneath the tree's raw roots, and I throw out
my hands until I skid to a stop

on my elbows. My son
has already turned toward the park,
having learned his way through this blueprint
of First Manassas, and cautiously

eyes the statue of Jackson,
whose stone chest furrows
from watching men fall to their deaths
at the First Battle of Manassas,

those whose names
crowd my sleep.
I too look up at Jackson
painfully from the battlefield's floor.

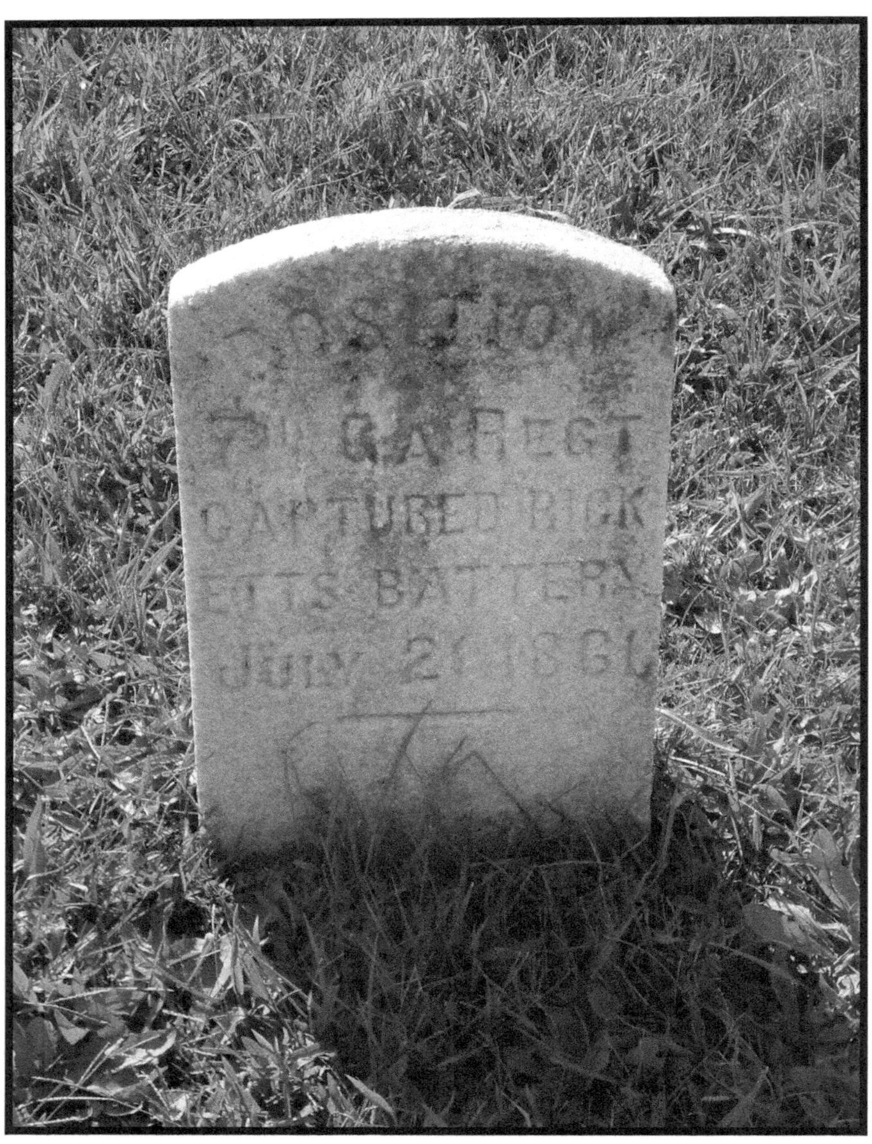
GA REGT
CAPTURED RICK

HEADSTONE

If I recall a time
trains carried cattle
of young men
to meet in these woods,

it is only in memory
of the darker times
that drag me here today.
In the shadow of an oak,

my son is the first to see
a grave marker
beside a stream.
If there were ever a time

trains carried a child and his rifle
to the foot of this tree,
the memory is burned
to the parched summer ground.

In the intermittent light of the forest,
I am the first to tell my son
how holes were made in the earth,
how the fallen were rolled over the cliff

and then covered with red earth,
how boys no older than he
were marked by a piece of stone.
If there were ever a time

memory should stop,
a time thought should not turn to word,
a time I should hold my son's narrow shoulders,
the curls of his hair,

the mind just beginning to form pictures
of young muscle shredded to bone
and bone blown to the air,
it must be here

among these trees
that tremble around us
like ragged flags from a war
my son will never forget.

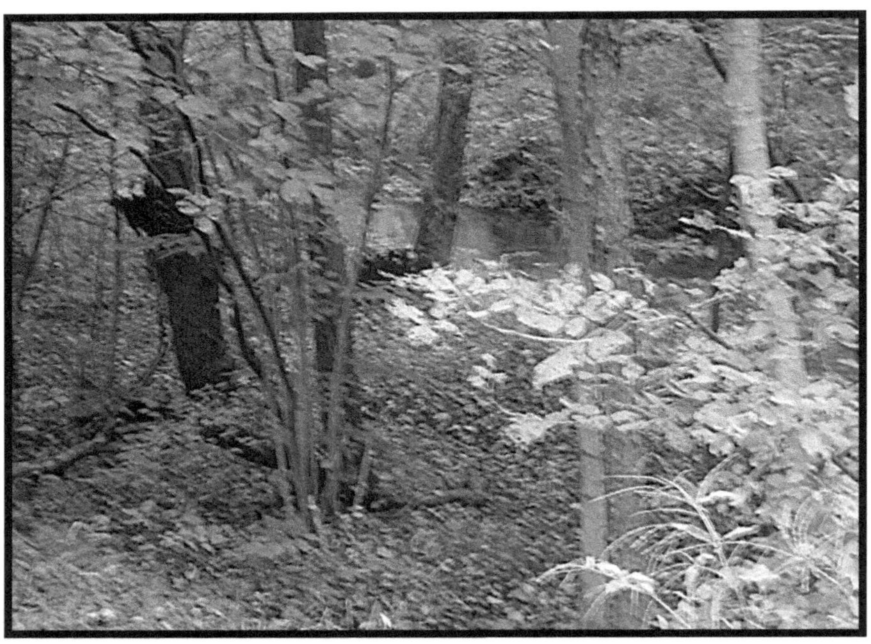

DEVIL'S FOX

Myth says it like this:
the origin,
the east bank of Bull Run,
was always shadow.
Sometimes at mid-day
when the shadow
seemed darkest,
odors of needled pines
blew over the creek,
and soldiers sensed life
in the shadow.

Dusk forced them together
when the shadow's chill
closed over Bull Run,
dusk when they heard devil's
fox swirl in hedges
and felt cold night
hang low enough
to touch their heads.

On that first chill
they scattered,
some hugging wild roots
for warmth,
others lying flat to the earth,
rising,
and galloping into the forest.

The next day
bits of flesh
would be found
on thorned bushes—
limp hanging leaves.

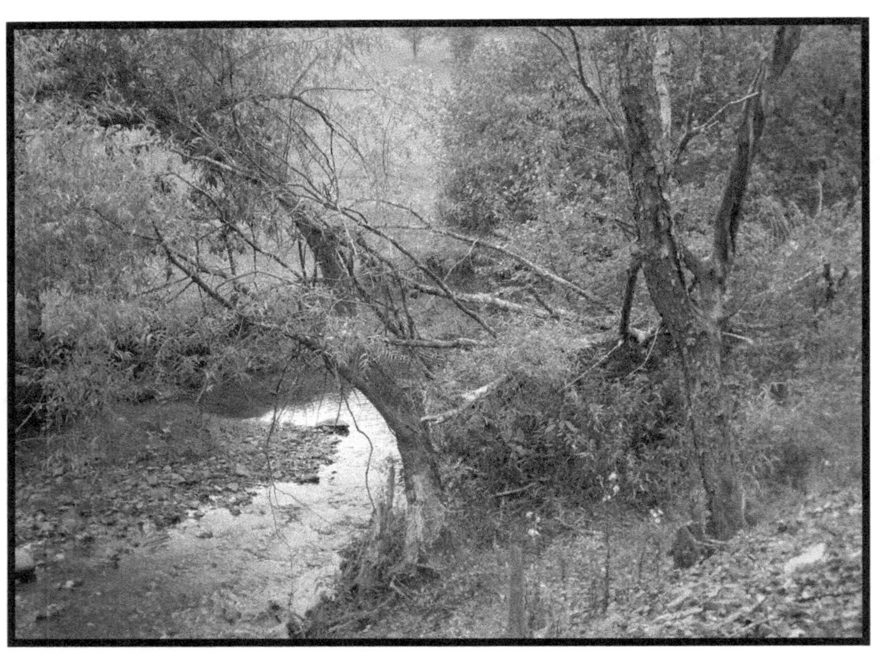

VIRGINIA SUMMER

for William Heyen

The silk scarf stretches
tightly across your face,
just long enough for you
to think you're dying.

These are the days
I've told you about, when
your bloodstream bursts
into your cheeks
and you run to the nearest pond
without care for snakes
sliding through undergrowth.

This is the stillness promised
to each of us, the silence
that sends us screaming
from our deepest dreams,
waking in the night,
alone and afraid.

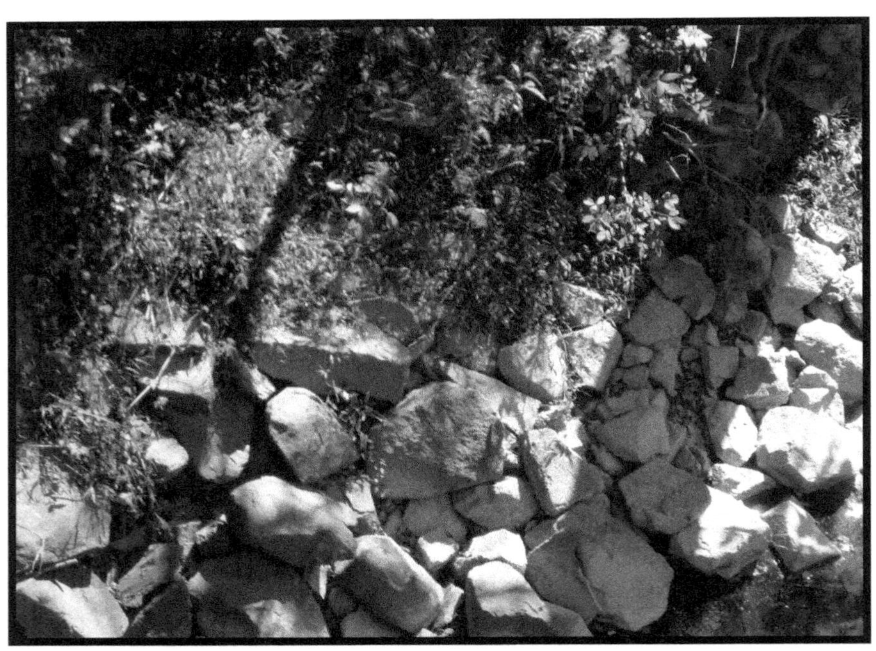

THE NEW START

Soldiers too prayed for rain
at first like penitents,
begging to begin—
again—fresh fluids floating
around them like indulgences.

They prayed for a holy rain,
the rain of forgiveness
that would lift them slightly
higher, a rain that would
leave the miracle of shadow
on the ground
where puddles ended,
shadows of angels they've believed in.

But rain does not fall
like the voices of politicians.
The noisy priests of war
do not dispense waters
to sustain us, our bodies, our earth.

Instead, soldiers that we are,
we grind clouds with every acid
breath, every carbon embrace
until we recognize our prayer
for something with gills and lungs,
something that will splash to shore.

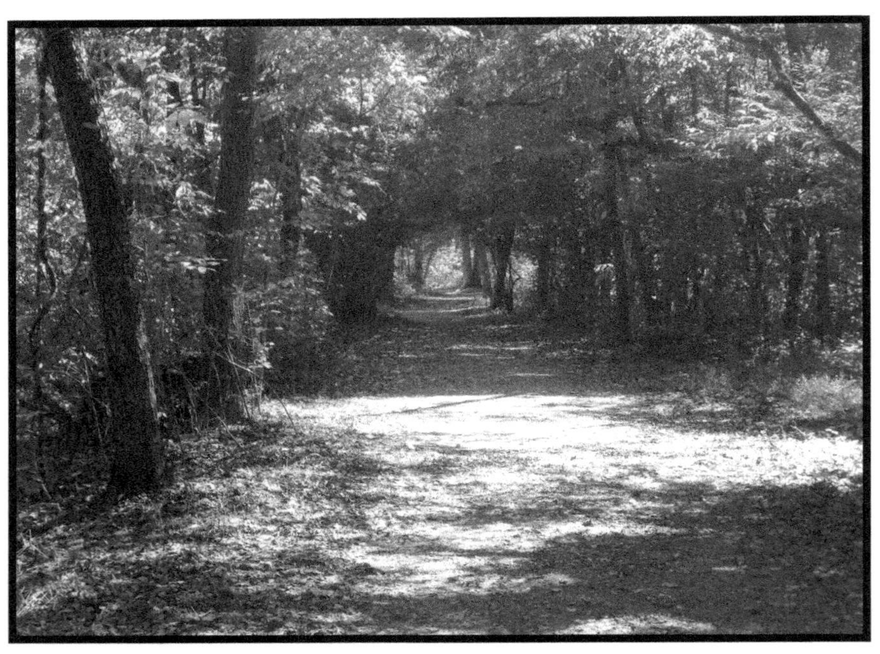

REMEMBERING JUNETEENTH

Something that we needed to do
has walked ahead of us. We're walking fast,
trying to catch up. Its footprints,
once hard in the earth, are soft
and fresh as we get closer.

This thing that demands to be done
waits ahead of us, now turns
and walks back to where we push against
the ground with our worn and tired feet.

Its sockets are empty. Its nostrils
flare at our scent. When we finally meet
we embrace like distant relatives.
We give it our eyes and help it to
the end of this long, unfamiliar road.

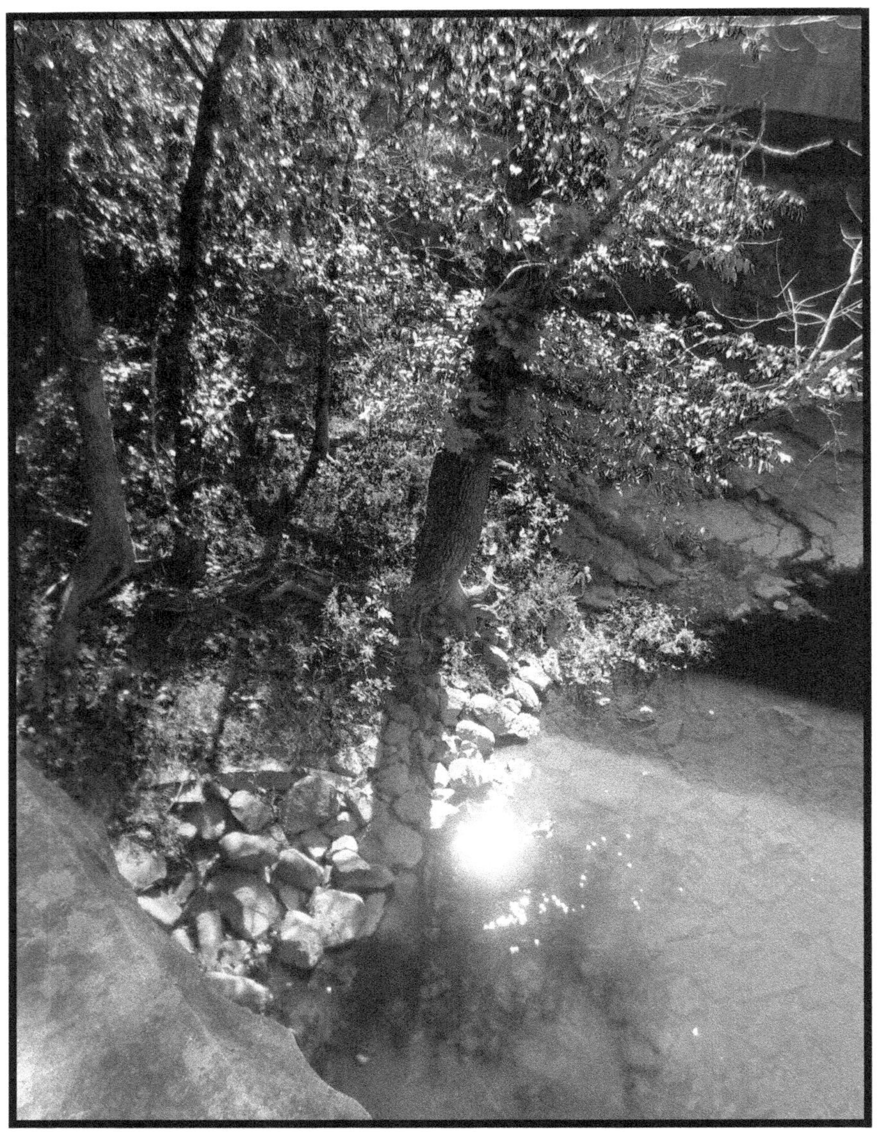

SWIMMING THE EARTH

Near Bull Run
where some summer days
you can walk from bank
to bank, keeping
your ankles dry,
I watched a dog swim
the mud.

Someone nearby called the dog,
but it continued to swim
on the tire tube of its body,
continued to crawl across
Bull Run.

We pointed and clapped,
we wiped our eyes and sat back.
The dog pushed on, its greedy
haunches rolling beneath it
until striking the bank,
falling into the grass
and its twisted tongue.

We laughed to our sides,
rolling down the opening hill
to the edge of Bull Run
where nothing ever stands as it might,
where even a dog
returning from water
smells of earth.

PART III: IN HOSTILE CLIMATES

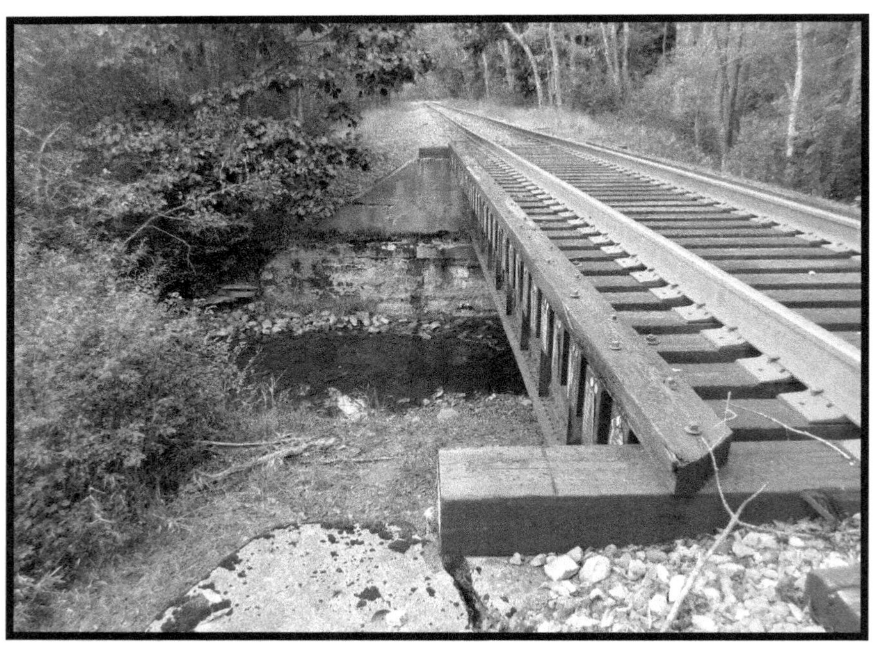

PASTE

You might have thought
I was making paste
with my feet in the mud.

Again you've found me
walking barefoot
through bone yards of the past.

If I tell you how often
I've made this journey
through the skull alone,

how often I've watched rain
level boundaries of my footprints,
you'd still hold before me

limbs of trees, leaves of flesh
left from passing carelessly
through the woods, alone, at night.

But this is no paste. Again
and again, I'm measuring my life
against footprints flooded by rain.

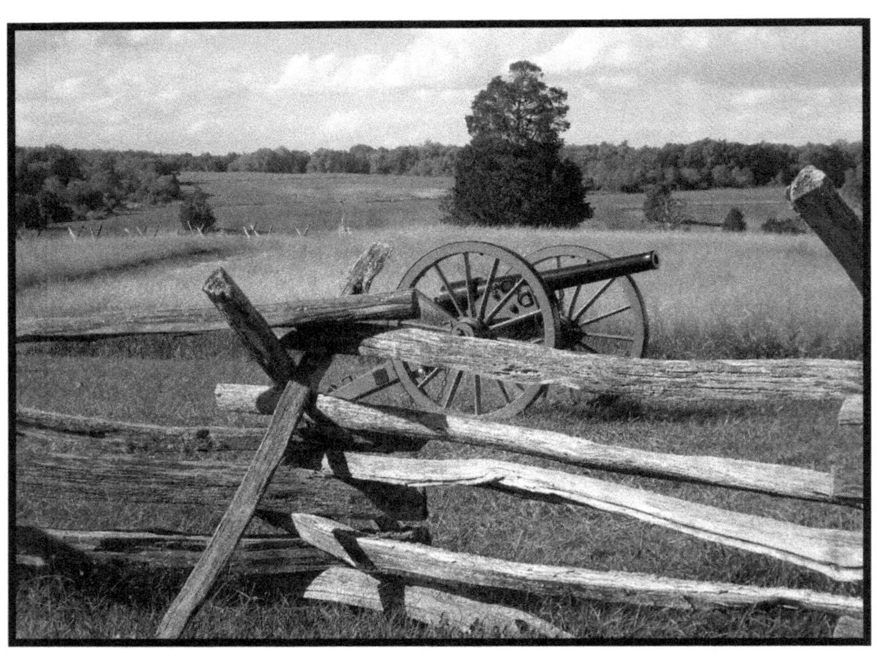

MANASSAS

On summer nights when
local sons of great grandsons
feast on plump grapes
slung like thumbs to the fence,
you'll hear a cry across the valley,
the cry you'd been told to ignore.

A woman picking wild berries
shouts for help, and you'll think
of the child strapped to her back,
of mud worms tunneling the bloodlines
of her legs, of body tattoos
burned for days to the earth.

You'll walk to the battlefield
and turn logs and bales
of dry grass to their sides
until you find the marks of her death
where they are surrounded by cannons,
where a child's tears are so small
they reach only to the tops of your shoes.

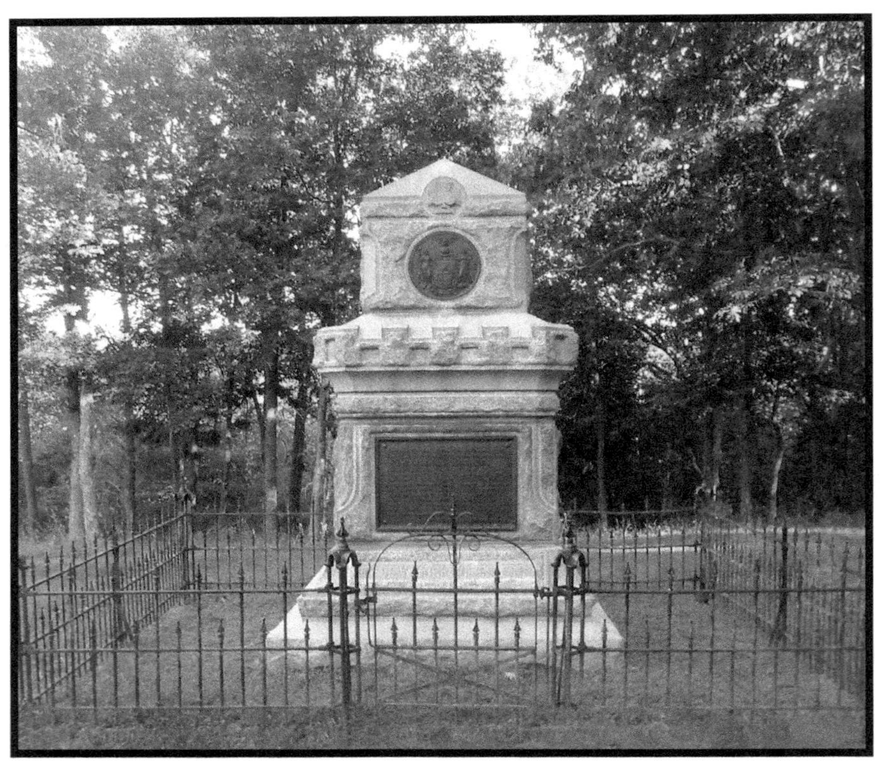

THE FIELD OF BATTLE

They rest in the fields like poppies.

Inscription on New York Monument, Manassas Battlefield

Now, volumes written, blood
long turned clay in Virginia earth,
I travel silent paths alone,
late at night,
flashlight in hand.

Silence around me
brings my eyes alert.
Nothing to hear except trees
brushing each other, dry grass
stiffening in late August heat.

I feel Manassas all around me,
in its deep pit of the past,
its sudden snap of wings through trees,
its heat so dense
I cannot escape it with my steps.

My body stiffens too
knowing this is the spot
of the New York Monument.
Here silence was broken
by shouts of young men
from my home
who came to war to wear uniforms
so bright colors preceded them
like a series of tiny warnings.

No one from New York
ever hid in these fields,
no one until now ever escaped.

Still, even I brush my forehead
and imagine in these deaths,
each man's skin turned dust,
each body feeling no greater heat
than at the moment of extinction.

I walk through these woods,
a monument to our past,
a tomb carrying within it
the murders committed,
the bodies in uniforms
pressed like poppies
between the pages
of this scrapbook
of First Manassas.

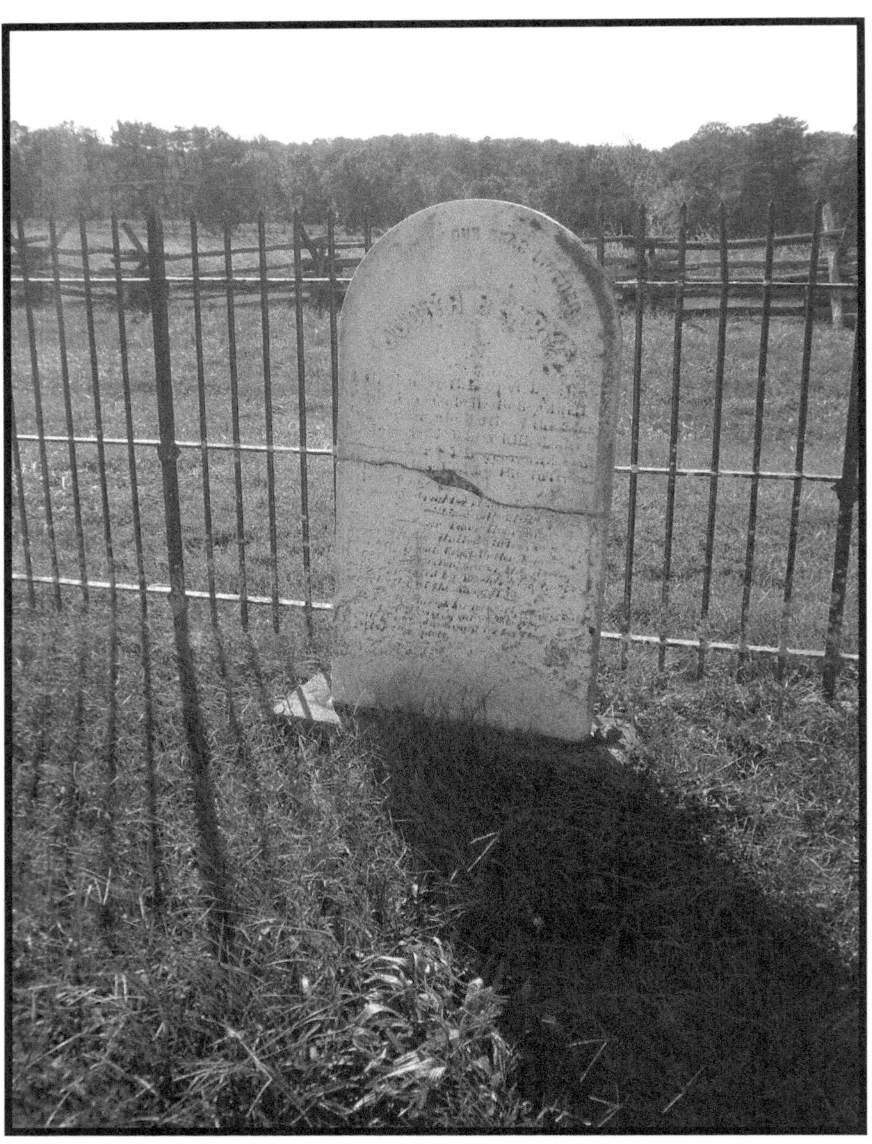

IN HOSTILE CLIMATES

A civilian tragedy took place in the Henry farmhouse. When the Federal attack began on the far side of the Warrenton turnpike, Mrs. Judith Henry, an aged bedridden woman, received five wounds from shell fragments and died soon after the battle.

Harry Hansen, The Civil War: A History

Mrs. Henry predicted weather
with her pain. Her fingers rang
with change, toes shook when she slept,
back buckled before rain.

She held weather beside her breast
the way others, in calmer climates,
held children in a salute of silence
and rest. It was not thunder or rain

that jolted Henry house
to the air above Bull Run. The changing
climate in the old woman's back-
yard could not force her down the hill.

She had not borrowed the land
the way others borrowed cash or time,
she was not a visitor to the hill.
Still, the sounds of muskets

exploded outside her house
like an old woman's anger.
Mrs. Henry knew sleep so deep
it took her near death.

Even in dreams she held Henry Hill
despite the incense of her parting flesh.
But in morning sunshine, she returned
from the dead and watched

from her bedroom window until, one day,
the weight of air ached inside her
and she knew how, in hostile climates,
change-weary women explode from within.

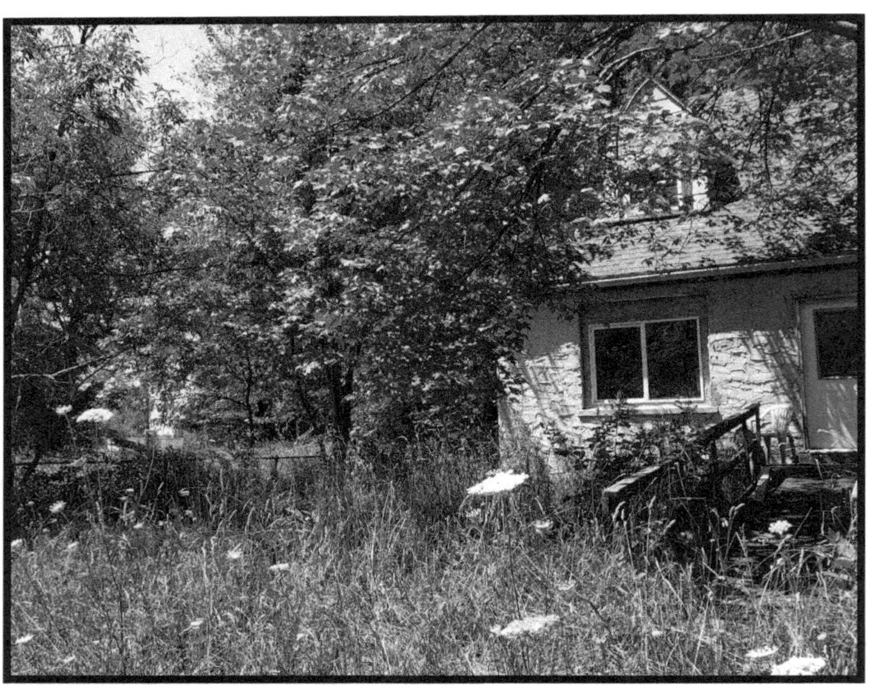

THE PATTERN OF SHADOWS

They crawled in through holes
in wood walls. All night
they ate, the kitchen
busy as smoke.

In the morning we cleaned
piles of dust
where they killed for last bits
of night and seeds of kitchen shadow.

Soon they were at our feet
and when we stepped to leave,
their backs cracked
beneath our heels.

We came back that night
to sounds inside the wall,
sounds so small we laughed.
But our laughs were followed

by other laughs, not our own.
And the walls darkened into
the long shadows of their bodies,
shadows with hands rolled into fists,

until there were no walls at all,
only shadows laughing their way toward us.
Then we stood
in the middle of the room,

our skin covering with lumps,
our skin,
like our lives,
filling with the pattern of shadows.

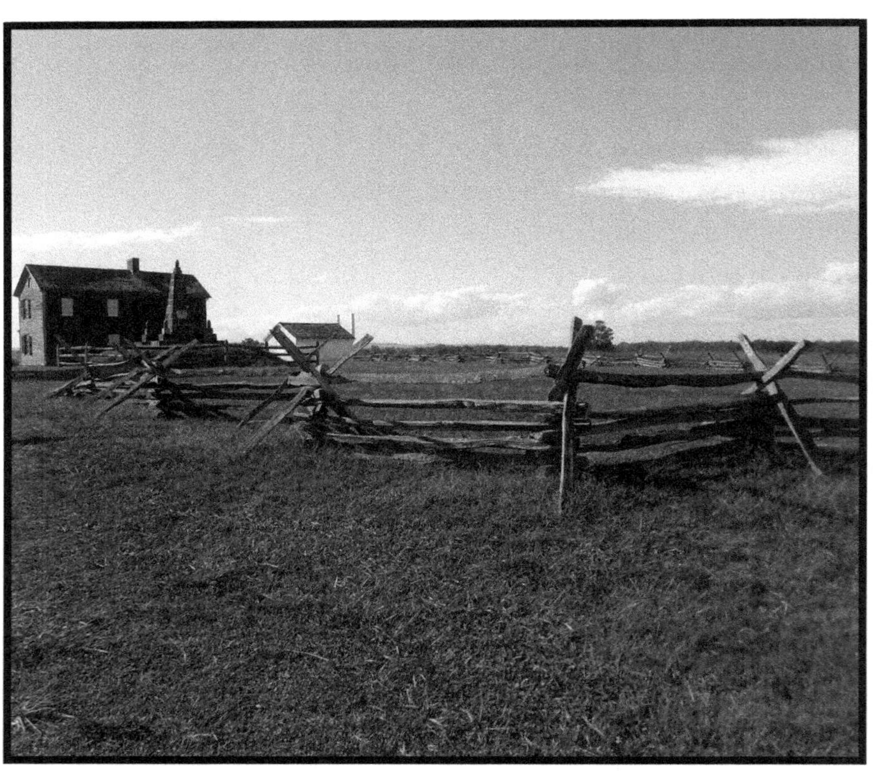

THE WATCHER

Between shed and fence,
in that narrow space behind my house
where old windows lean in tall weeds,
something lives, something larger

than a man. It walks at night,
lifting each discarded window
and peering through.
I did not live here then.

But I know, in gray days
when those windows fit this house,
an old man creaked these floors,
when floors were made of pine.

Some nights I hear him downstairs,
moving his heavy feet
from study to kitchen and back.
Some nights the desk chair sighs

as if the man, in ghostly play,
has spun his weight.
I've locked the doors
and removed that old glass

from behind the shed. Still,
each night after locking myself in,
I walk to my bedroom window and watch
as a castle of a man moves

from battlefield to shed
to stare inside my house
at a past that follows me
whenever I sleep.

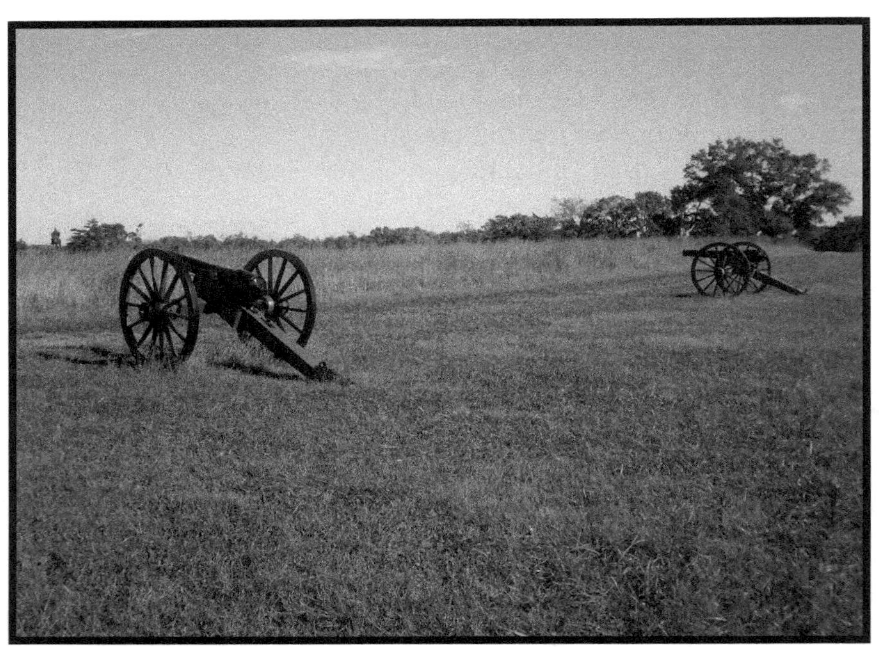

THE SEARCHER

A soldier I can only hear
walks through my yard,
grass silences cracking like splintered
wood against his boots.

He walks a forest where cannons once
traveled in wagons on dirt roads
and hundreds of tired men searched silently
through undergrowth for places to hide.

Late at night, the searcher's feet
shout against the grass, grass caverns echo
every sound. He walks through my yard,
boots whistling away his fears.

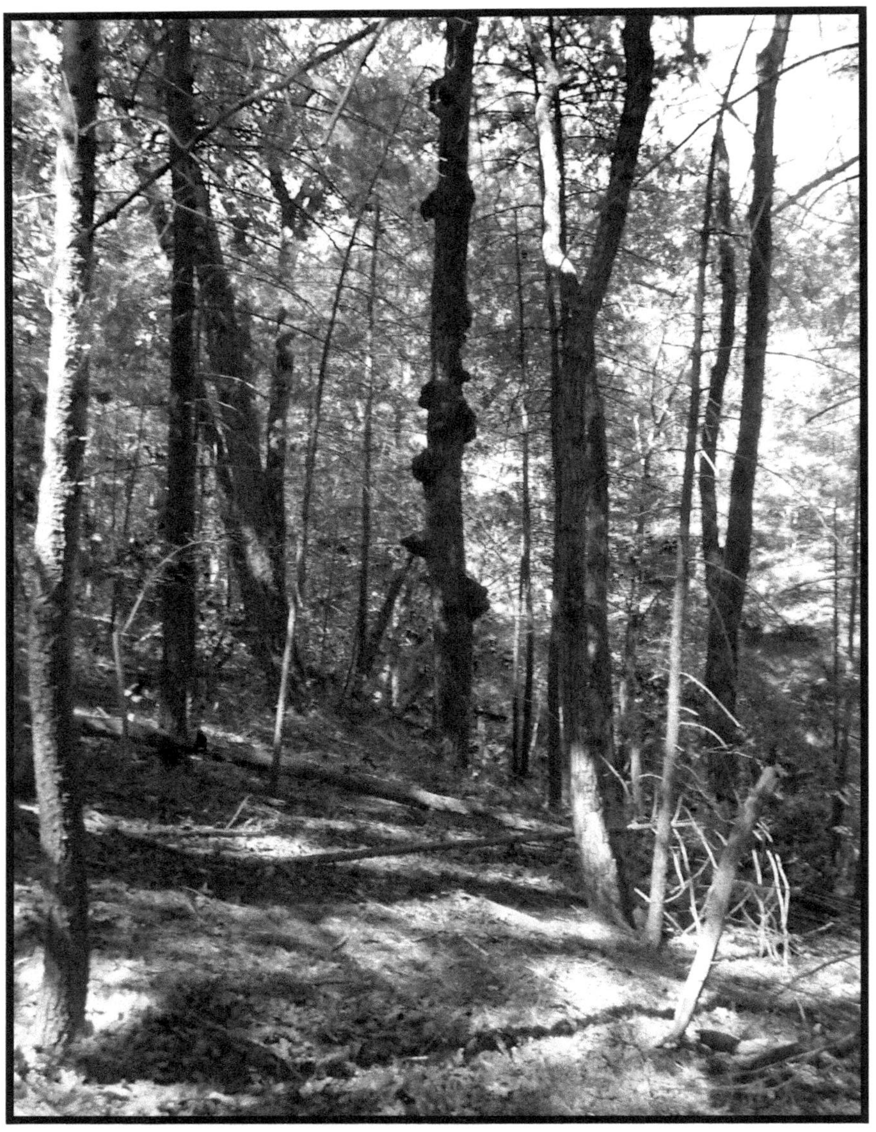

THE SEASON OF FROZEN LIMBS

In this season of frozen limbs,
a soldier staggers through the battle-
field, rifles hooked to his coat.

Some say this is not a man at all,
limping deeper into the forest,
deeper into the Manassas of his nightmares.

On nights when his cries whirl through
leafless trees, he presses his heavy beard
against lighted windows in houses nearby.

His cry weeps against the window,
weeps from inside a torn cape. Late at night,
my daughter pulls a blanket over her head

to muffle the sound of wind rushing
against her window, the explosion of birds
unfolding against a background of trees.

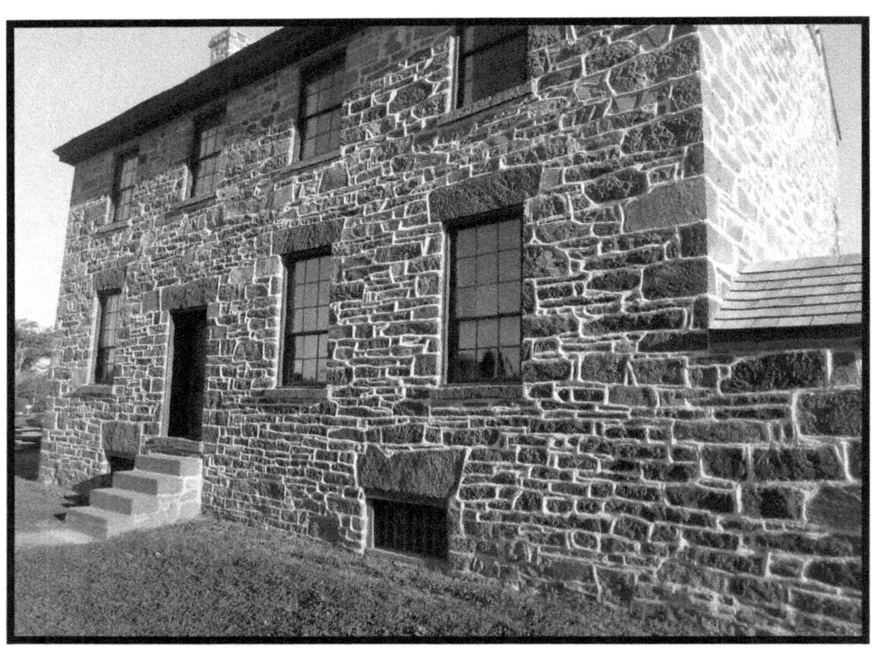

THE GREETER

Early morning, summer in Manassas,
humidity a tangle of haze.
In the distance curtains open.
Sunlight picks up specks
of dust that rise with the family,
trying to leave.

A young woman pulls on a pink slip,
the outline of her body
waving in the mirror.
Her children lie in bed,
dreaming of summers at camp,
singing around the fire

and of stories about the battlefield
ghost who glows at night—the Greeter,
they call him—who bows and smiles
and tells them with his arms held out
that they are here, in the year
of his death, holding a rifle
against their shoulders,
running into him with a sword,
thrusting through their fear
and pulling until dark.

The woman knows
but has no one to tell
how, late at night,
from the field beside her house,
she has seen shadows move forward
until they fade in the glow
of her daughter's window.

She has heard sounds in her yard
of empty shoes
filling with moon.

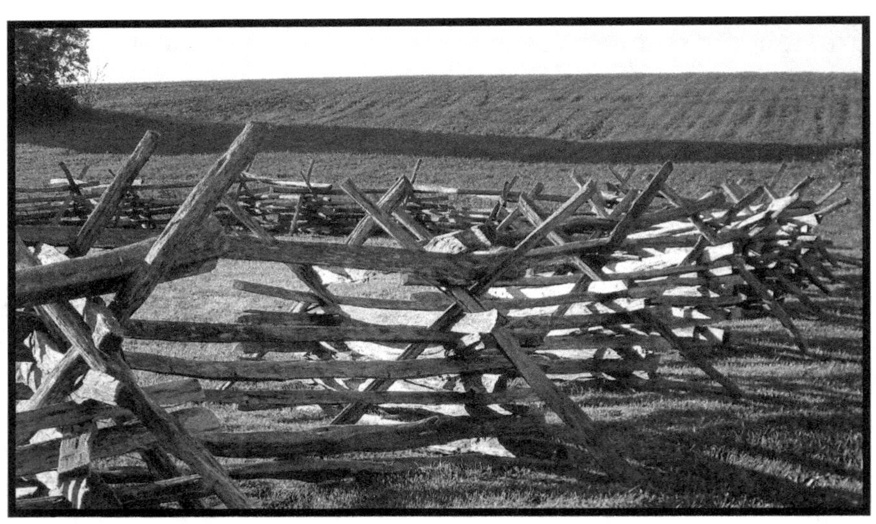

A LADDER OF LIGHT

for Krissy

My daughter hugs a pillow of dream.
When the past comes to her,
it comes slowly,
in glimpses outside the clock's circle.

When she sleeps, something always comes up.
Not the sun. Not the thumb
begging its way down turnpikes
of gravel promises.

Something always comes up in past tense,
like the memory of a man dragging
his long legs to rope swings in backyards
of perfectly-shaped childhoods.

I know she doesn't dream randomly.
I imagine her dreaming of the man
I've never seen, who lifts his scaled face
toward the lighted bedroom where she sleeps.

Her window slants into the yard
a ladder of light so fragile
only the dead can climb it
on nights when the moon shivers behind clouds.

I worry about the pasts
a child carries into this life.
I worry about my daughter's dreams,
the way they recoil in the morning.

Once I thought only the old
threw memories into a sack,
carrying them like the tramp
who loads the top of his back.

But when the moon begins to shake
above trees beyond my fence,
moving slowly in a circle
it never completes,

my daughter stands at the top
of her night light's ladder,
looking at a landscape the moon remembers
and whispers to her when she sleeps.

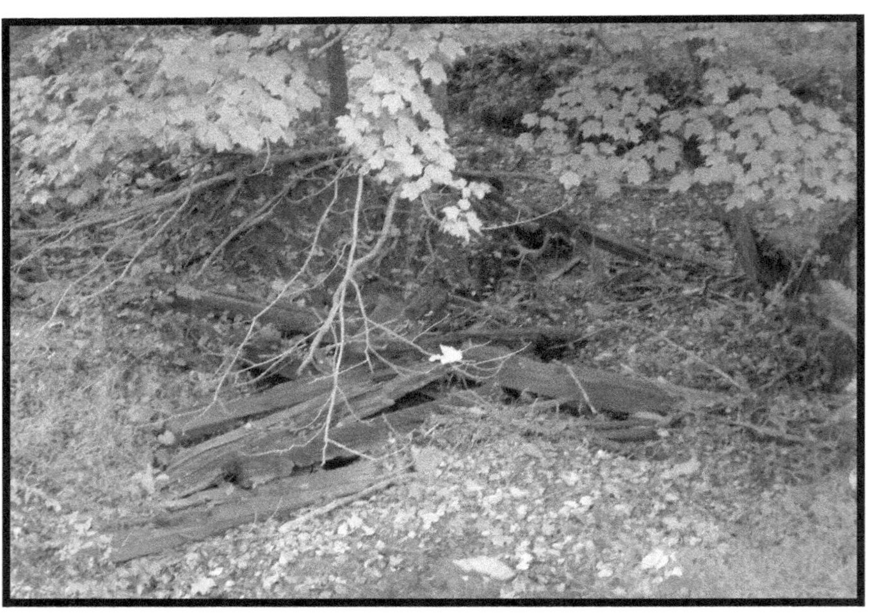

THE BATTLEFIELD'S WINTER

Last night, snow dropped
a speckled net
above the pines.
Today, wind carves
delicate curves
even poor men
can walk through.

Whatever fell during the night
knew this morning
I'd measure my steps
so cautiously, so slowly,
silent streams would shake
beneath them,
shallow graves protected
from my timid weight.

Even the deer
that walked circles in the dark
pressed maps more firmly
with his feet.
It is no wonder
I can't read them.

No one is sadder
than a man who walks alone,
missing the snow at his feet,
the trails where no one will know come spring
how lost men have been in these woods.

Now, far from the battlefield's winter,
I remember deep snows
I've walked and how, with one courageous
step, I dropped my weight
into a drift,
and felt it shudder and give way
as though I would be
the first to know
the direction of water,
the direction of cold.

PART IV: VIOLENCE

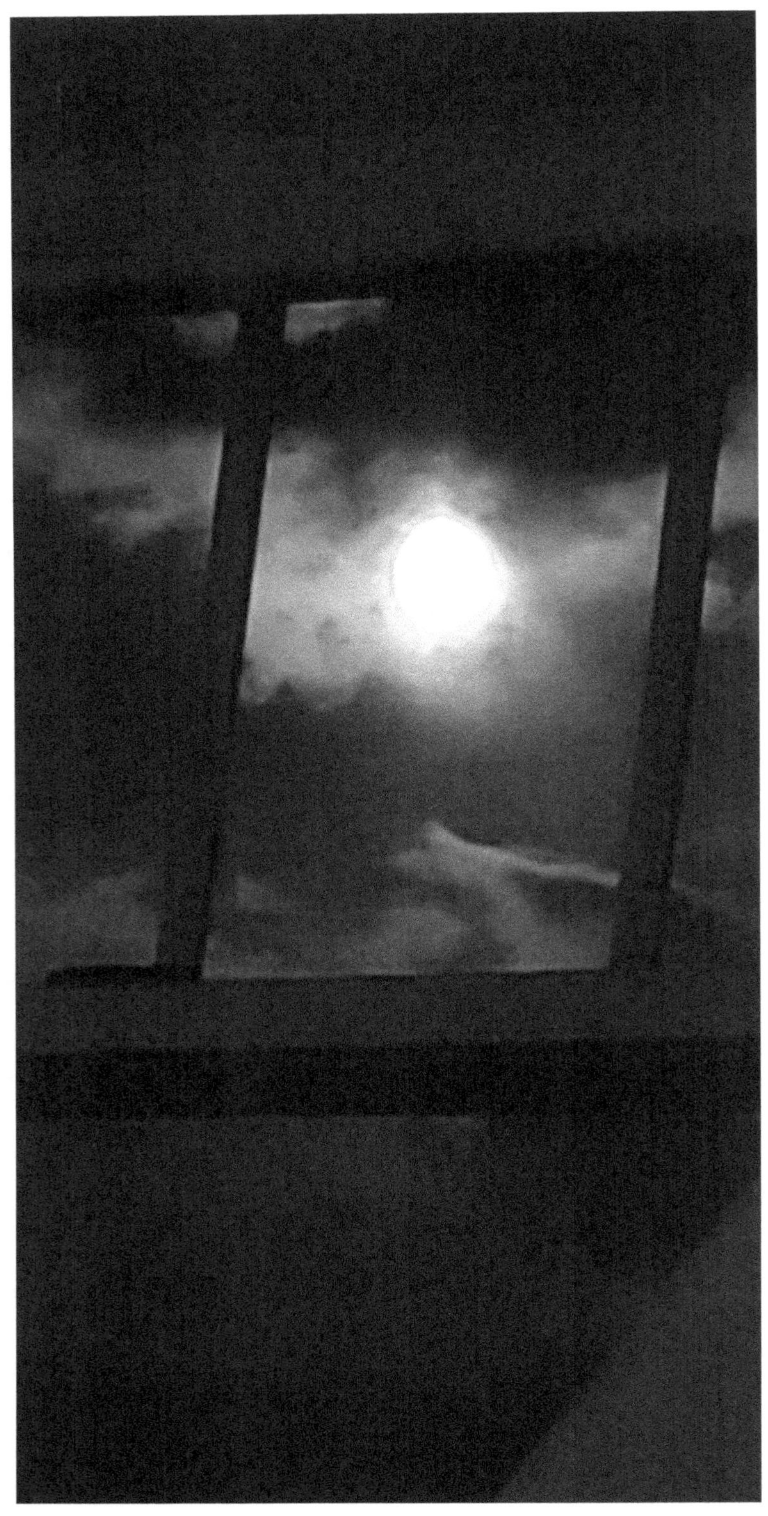

VIOLENCE

1.

A man never knows
what will happen
if someone places a gun
in his hands.
Will fingers freeze
on the trigger
and skin tear
when the hand is pried from steel?
Will long shadows
press closer together
into the corner of the room
until someone decides?
This is murder.
I will do it.
Over and over again,
I will do it.

2.

Maybe you're walking
down the street
when you hear something metal
slip through the hole in your pocket.
You keep walking until
you hear it again.
You wonder what, in this life,
could so strongly want
to be lost. A coin,
a gold filling from
the newly dead?

Maybe you're walking
down the street
when you hear someone
call your name.
And when you turn,
it's your son,
carrying his best memories of you
in a box the size of his thumb.
And the sound of metal
hitting the sidewalk,
of something trying so hard
to be lost in this lifetime,
follows you home and calls you
father. With all his might,
calls you father.

3.

There are men who keep violence
by their beds all night
as though they can prevent
their dreams.
I knew a man who slept
with a knife under his pillow.
Once when his wife returned
with a cup of water, he jumped
at her from the shadows,
the knife shining beneath her throat
like the eyes of blind men.

And when he turned back
to his sleep, he dreamed
of children stabbing
the backs of their hands
with sharpened pencils
until blood rushed
to the ground. All around them
a halo of gray shouted
from the dream, and he awoke
jabbing the backs of his
hands with the knife.

4.

I know you haven't listened
since the beginning.
This talk of violence
eating the hearts
of children and frightened
old men who, like me,
take their terror with warm
milk and a bit of chocolate.

But there are corners of the room
filled with hours
no one has named,
colors only the blind know
and shades so subtle
we call them black.

There's smoke right now
curling to the top of this page,
smoke drowning someone's last shout,
the shout we all hear when
deep in our dreams
our lovers whisper in our ears.
Right now there are fingernails chewed
to the flesh,
blood slowly driven to the surface.
And there are men throwing
their wives through windows
and women beating their children.
And there are children

dancing around us,
their faces pink and bloated,
their lips moving
like triggers, slowly,
cautiously, aiming at you.

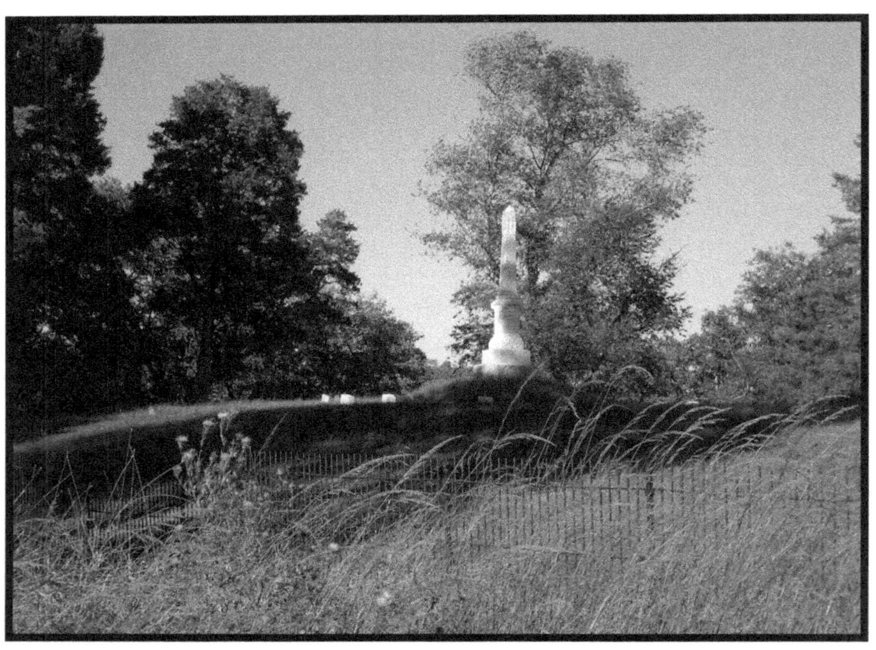

WAR PLANS

[I]t was common knowledge that there would be dancing at Fairfax Court House after the Northerners had driven the Southerners back to Richmond.

V. C. Jones, First Manassas

Plans made, thoughts already easing
into victory at Manassas,
women were sent to Fairfax,
women with hair pinned into buns
and packed into flowered hats.
Soldiers dancing around them danced
the dust, danced the heat.

And with each step, dust exploded
the air, heat boiled the skin
until pellets the size of tears
rolled to the forehead,
danced to the ground.

There would be dancing
through the streets and in the courthouse,
a war plan that would surely take
Confederates by surprise.
Part of the plan: hoop marks
on the ground. Part of the plan:
perfumed ties tucked into collars.

A young soldier's feet ached from
the thought of so much dancing,
so he leaned back on the ground
into the flesh of meshed knuckles.

No one dances dreams of death.
No one plans “a monster military
picnic” and carries blood’s tools
down Warrenton’s Pike.
No one brushing dust from a musket
polishes the barrel with plans.

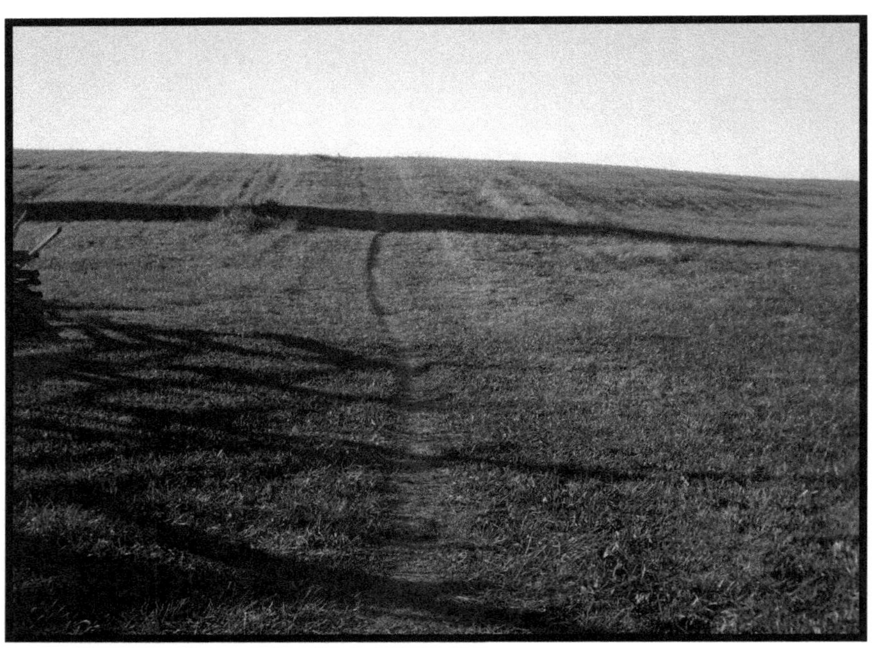

WAITING FOR THE FLOOD

Parents watched,
crossing bony fingers for luck.
Sunrise, and children step
into the hoarse throat of despair
their fathers have carried like muskets.

The old know to bow.
Even young sunlight returns
the flood of their eyes.
Together they stand on Matthew's Hill
above Bull Run
twisting leather flesh
into baskets of prayer.

To one side of the hill,
tiny bird wings of pain
flutter in the dark.
On the open field,
sunrise spreads over
layers of haze
softly as fingers fall apart,
silently as prayers slip
from lips. The children's eyes
open like graves.

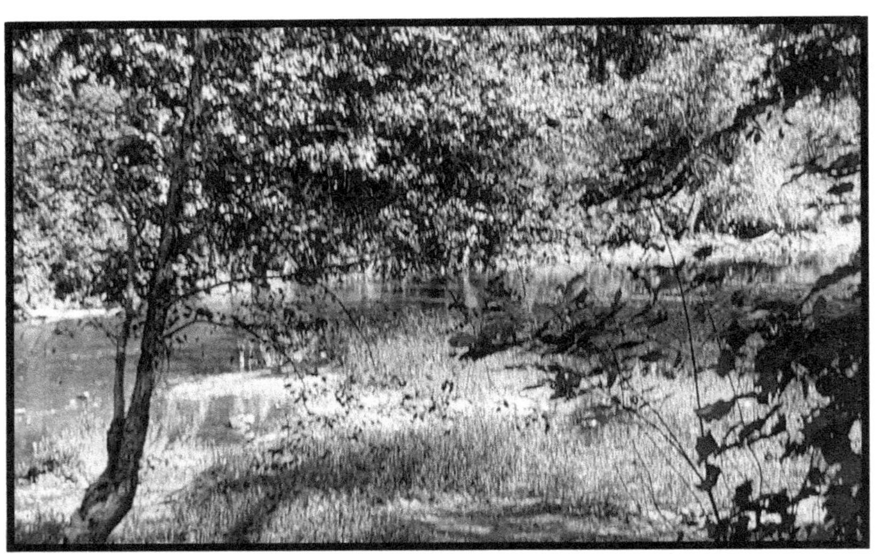

A COUNTRY PATH, MANASSAS BATTLEFIELD

To give the artillery clear command over the approaches [General Beauregard] had caused trees to be felled.

Harry Hansen, The Civil War: A History

There's a path
in the battlefield—
a crease through oaks—
leading to private land
and a lake.

You can't tunnel the path
with a car.
So you walk
through wild grass
toward trees
where moss swings hang
like honey loops.

Dew fills tiny
callous holes
in your feet.
Oak canes grow flesh
in your hands.
The forest
is the blueprint
of an animal.

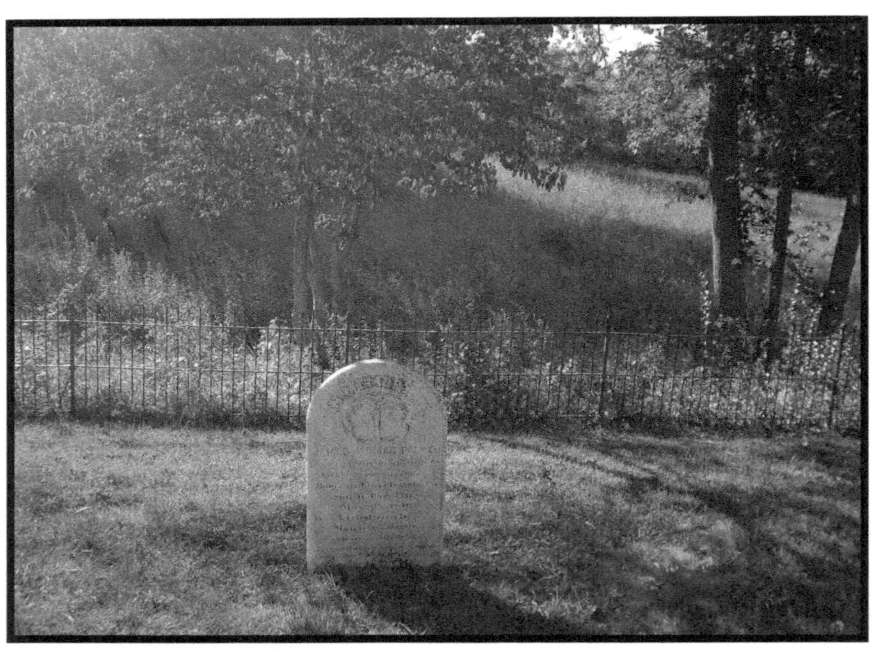

CLARENCE CAREY

a little eight-year-old from Alexandria. As soon as the Colonel's back was turned, off [Clarence] went for his musket.

The Battle of Bull Run

There's a world where
muskets melt in the mud,
a place where bullets bounce
from the breast like berries.

There's a world where a child's
dreaming eyelids tremble,
forcing a death, a fire among
trees, a family to move.

In this world, everything stops.
Children wake to the nursery,
the sweet smell of new wood,
the soft warmth of thick blankets.

Even children far from war
dream the boot's deep drum. The lonely child
at the back of an attack
walks the hidden curve of hills.

But when a boy is taken
into a dream that's not his own,
a dream that plays on despite
the closing eyelid's darkness,

he enters the war at Bull Run
as though sometime soon the curtain
will rise, and he will wake to watch
dust escape through sunlight.

In his hands he might take
a warm rifle, feel its weight,
its shape, its sudden thrust
against soft shoulder flesh.

He follows in this dream,
waits until no one watches,
until even the colonel collides
with the living and the dead.

In that collision, the musket
rubs the boy's finger red,
and a soldier, at the rifle's point,
flutters against a bullet.

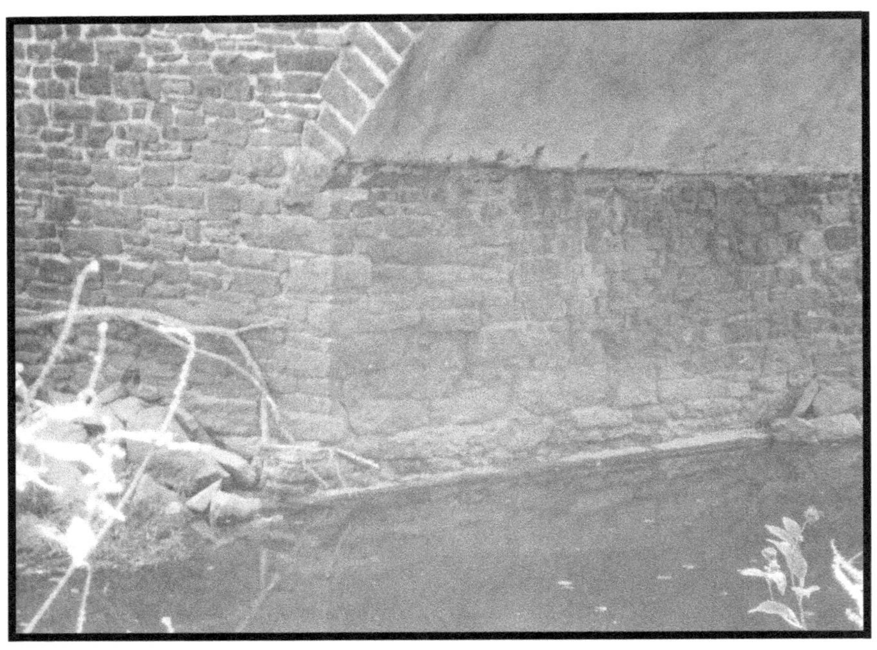

SURGICAL FEVER

It was usually the ensuing infection which caused death. The so-called "surgical fevers."

Medicine of the Civil War *pamphlet*

There's a space, some say, called the soul,
a place wounded by weapons and war,
scarred when the surgeon wrings his red hands
into anonymous pools, knee deep on dirt floors.

There's a soreness deep inside,
a fever passing silently through
the living like August wind
through tall Manassas weeds.

There's a spot on the soul
that ledgers the loss
in shapes nightmares take
when the moon throws its aimless

weight through trees and to the ground.
So, the living feel sad
when stiff metal blades shatter bone,
sorrow when legs splatter

to the floor, remorse when fevers
rise until their pitch stitches pain
to the tender edges of their ears.
So, we say, "better this

than the deep death of our souls,"
but stand knee deep anyway
in still rivers of what once must have been
people we've only read about.

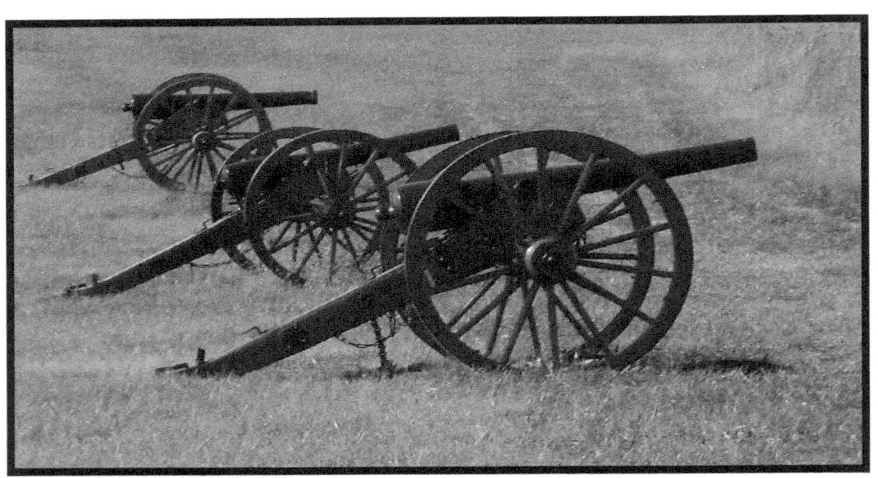

PROVISIONS

Another delaying factor was a 30-pound Parrott gun attached to Tyler's division. It was to open the firing at Stone Bridge and might even turn out to be the deciding factor, for it was looked upon as a mighty weapon.

V.C. Jones, First Manassas

Soldiers in front tuck away fear
like provisions they'll draw from tomorrow.
Their horses swallow miles
of hills and dust. Chickens, too slow
to lunge aside, explode into feathers
on the road. But when soldiers pull up short
to rest, to wait for the walking young
to fill in behind, even the earth suffers
jolts and shocks of delay. War waits

for the child's bones to harden,
waits for feelings to flatten against
boot heels. Soldiers up front wait
for the weary to walk roads of despair
so thick feet pull from the ground,
legs vibrate limp-kneed in wool pants,
arms swell beneath the weight of heat
rising in waves on the road ahead.

Even the hot brain, planning tomorrow's war,
hisses in the sun. Cold shocks of Bull Run
send shivers of Confederate laughter to shore.
And the Yankee soldiers gather in moonlight
to wait for the "mighty weapon"
as they sit through this delay, pulling
a small parcel of fear from their packs,
passing it from mouth to mouth.

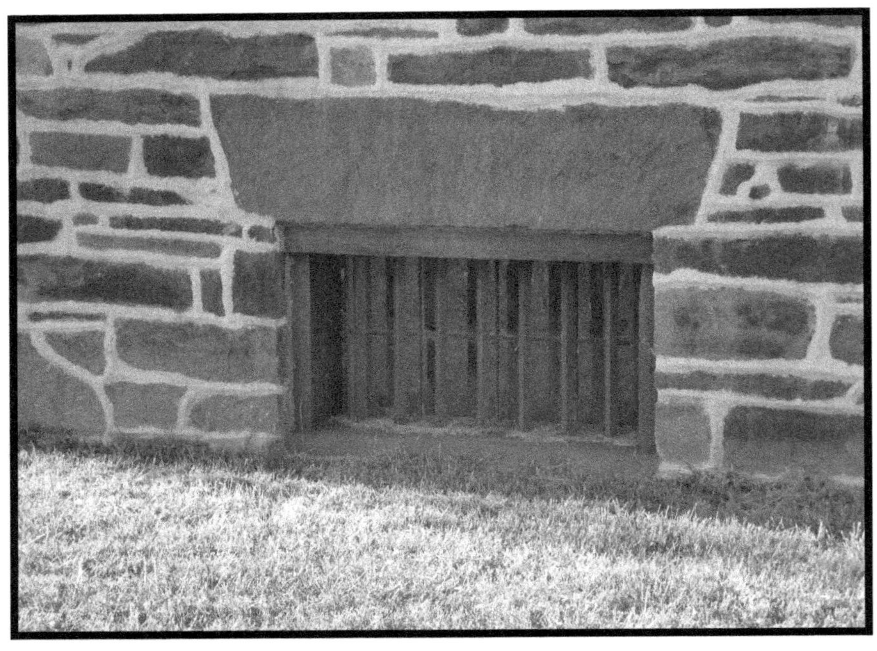

VOICES

A light slashes through clouds.
A horse's blindness is tossed
aside and driven into the night.

Voices of grown men are thrown
to the brown earth, turning
over and over like a swarm of bees.

I hear trees
call to the lightning, begging
to return to buds.

I hear the numb sounds of rain
against my window. Old cracks in the walls
sigh like wooden lungs. I'm cold

beneath the blankets, my arms outstretched,
face buried in pillow, my ears red and sore
where they are licked by the voices.

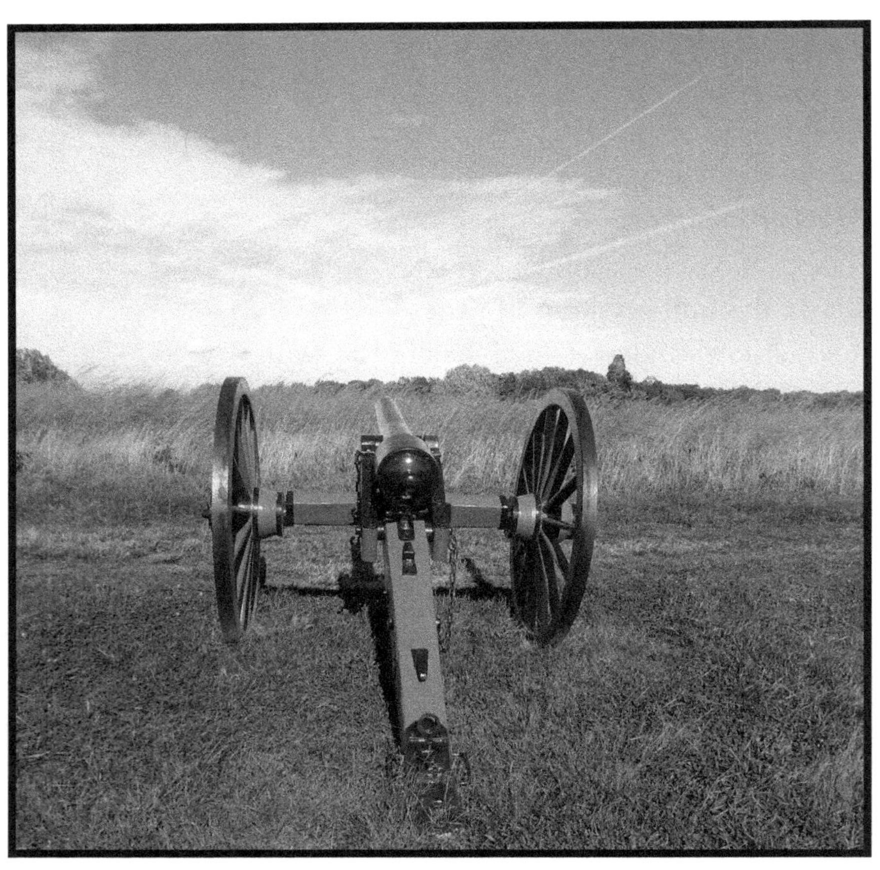

A PLAN OF ACTION: GENERAL IRVIN MCDOWELL

General McDowell was a native of Ohio, forty-three years old, who was graduated from West Point Military Academy in 1838 and had served with distinction on the staff of General Winfield Scott in the Mexican War. General Scott asked McDowell to draw up a plan of action against the Confederate position at Bull Run.

Harry Hansen, The Civil War: A History

McDowell knew the way air
planted in the ground
turned a harvest of flesh.
Instructed to do so,

he planned a war in Manassas so short
no one would remember.
Even then, men in their last days
of bondage to bayonet,

men with women and children
waiting in the dense cover
of the North,
would turn from the odor of smoke

and run until tendons
tore through their flesh,
run through Manassas farmland,
through land welted from the plow

as though the earth's soft skin
might surprise the sudden boot.
This was land flooded in spring,
streams so thick

with immeasurable distances,
the odor of lighted homesteads rose
to tree level and tore Bull Run
into lonesome lanterns

limping in the night.
McDowell came to know lanterns, leaving,
twisting through trees, a surgeon's knife
cutting through the flesh of war.

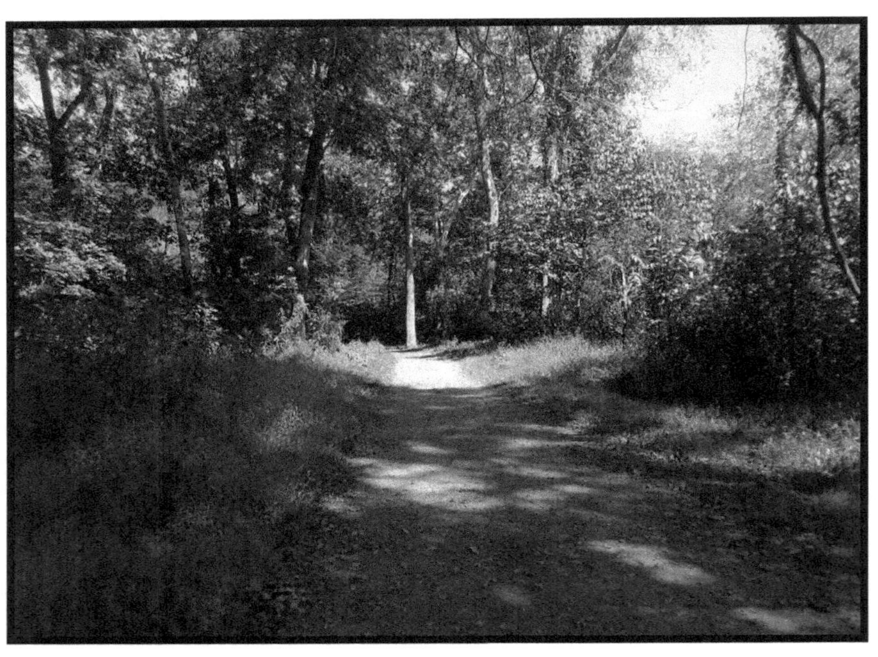

DESERTERS

The first Battle of Bull Run showed that it would take months of stern discipline to harden the farm hands, store clerks, bookkeepers, brakemen, and teamsters so that they would stand in the face of fire.

Harry Hansen, The Civil War: A History

They begin their march toward home
unexpectedly at first,
surprised themselves
to feel packs on their backs.

Once in the cover of the woods
they understand they have planned all along
to stretch out one leather-soled trudge,
then another, until puffs of dust rise

rhythmically to their nostrils,
easy at first as early morning ballet.
Later, miles from camp and hungry, when wind
shoves against their struggling forms,

they learn what the miner knows
when he lifts himself from the pit,
feeling all over
the weight of his body, the strength of air.

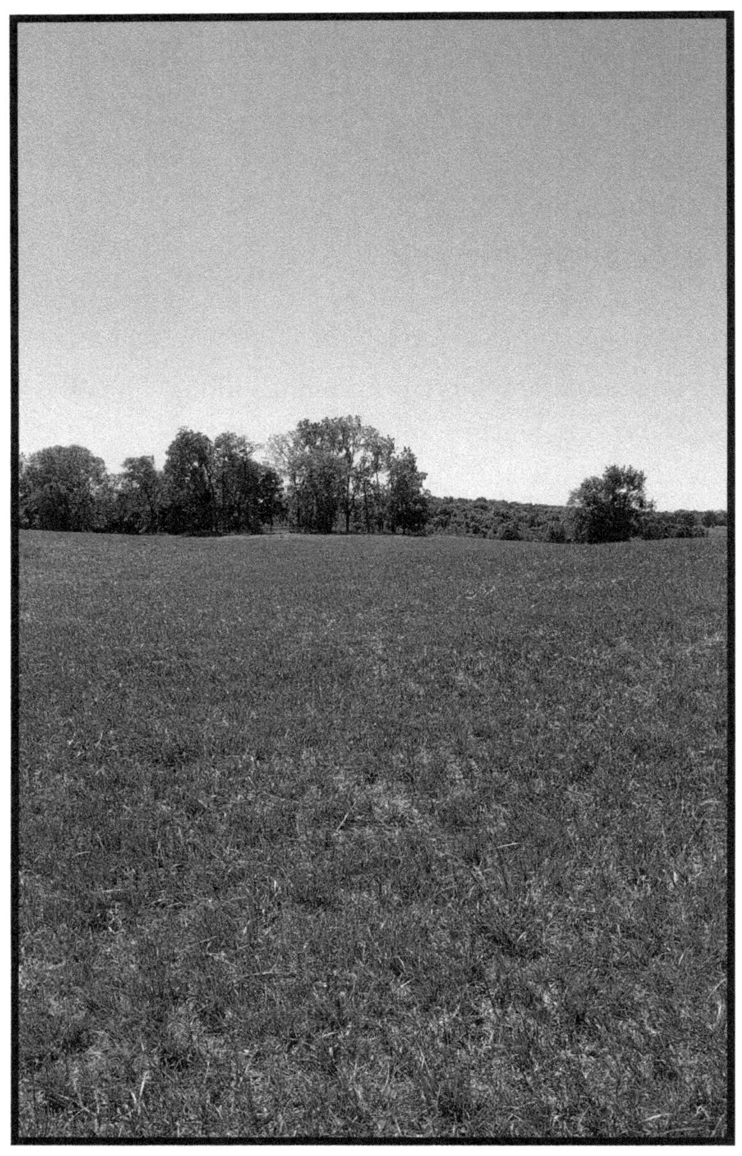

A MURAL OF WAR: E. P. ALEXANDER

On a thirty-odd foot tower near Manassas a signal officer would stand and wig-wag Boy Scout fashion an important message.

V.C. Jones, First Manassas

Soft wood bent
beneath Alexander's weight
as he pulled himself
step by step into newer bodies,
each heavier than the last.

We have all been there,
climbing with him
in our dreams, watching death
shed its scaly skin.

Though the dream splinters,
history opens
into a field
beneath a thirty-foot tower
where bodies move, so small
Alexander imagined
filling his palm with them.

Closing his eyes, he'd strip
tiny limbs to bones
whitening at his feet
in the blare of the next day's sun.

He stood so distant,
so high as he watched,
men floated into patterns beneath him,
stripes against tall June wheat,

filling the woods in such easy strokes
he would describe their movements later
in the painter's words.

Once men were locked in place,
he moved his body,
holding arms overhead in prayer,
then at his sides like wings
of some long-extinct, flightless bird.

Someone at the base of Matthew's Hill
understood the long strokes of movement—
Look out for your left; you are turned, he said—
and painted for General McDowell
a picture of men mounted into patterns,
unraveling into trees,

patterns I understand
when I dream of wars long gone,
bodies encased in clay
and an artist who stroked a canvas with his arms
as though painting for others
a mural of war.

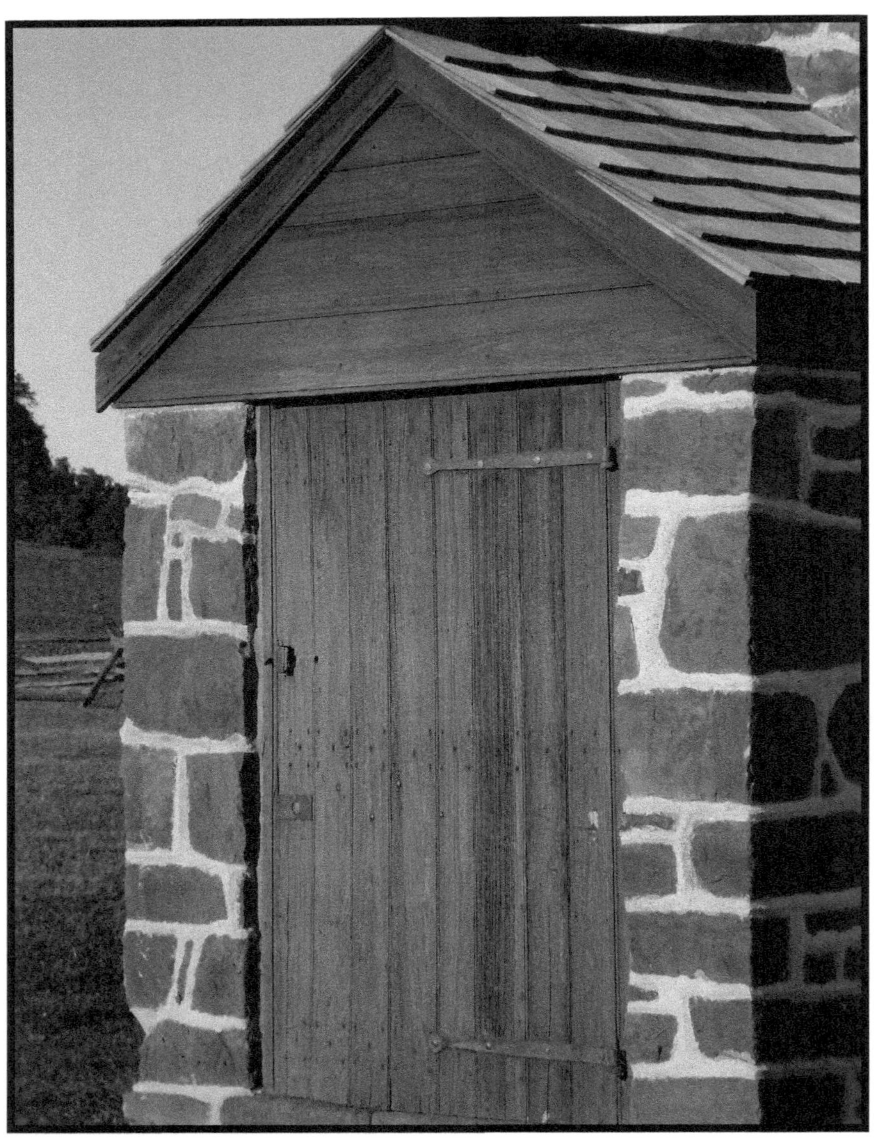

SMILING PUBLIC MAN: A PORTRAIT OF GENERAL DANIEL TYLER

McDowell instructed Tyler to "keep up the impression that we are moving on Manassas."

Harry Hansen, The Civil War: A History

the children's eyes
In momentary wonder stare upon
A sixty-year-old smiling public man.

W. B. Yeats, "Among School Children"

He works at making a smile
the way others work at making
a living. There are days,
he knows, when the wooden lip
will not bow, days when no arrow
will fly from his mouth.

Walking into a room,
you might find him,
lips forced upward,
cowering like a prisoner
in the corner of a cold cell,
unshaved and weeping,
limp as the ragged line of sweat
sagging above his mouth.

Other days, he takes form
in light blasting
through his window. On his spine
you see the treadmill of vertebrae,
the curved blossoms of despair.

Yet, he turns, a "smiling public man"
with teeth so white,
so formally introduced to each other,
you'll stop to notice how nicely his eyes
fit the curve of his cheekbones,
how delicately the curtain
of his forehead
shades his eyes.

And in his eyes,
if you look closely enough,
you'll see an old man
walking alone
on a moonless night
into the fog of his own breath.

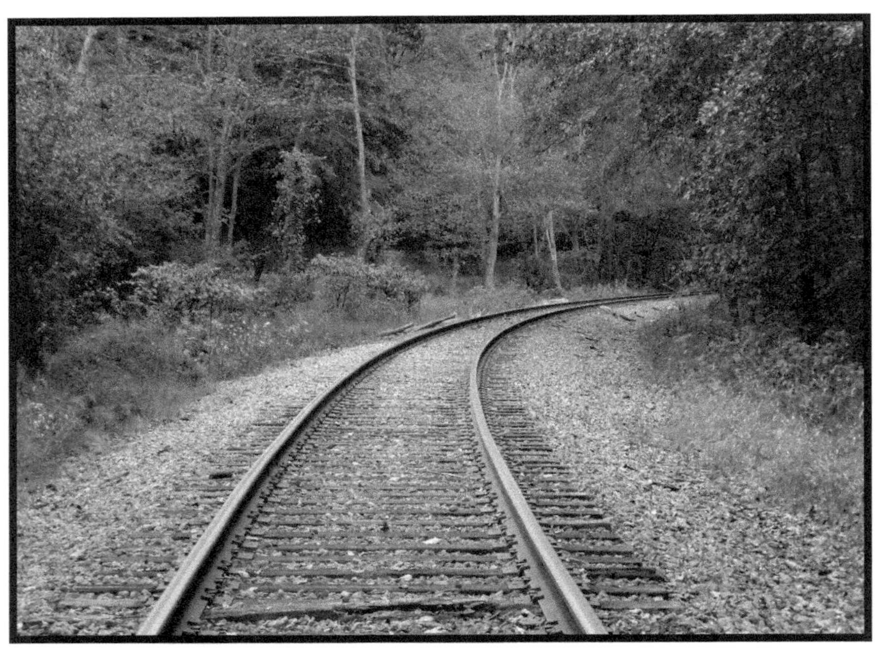

TRAVELING BY TRAIN THROUGH MANASSAS

Traveling by train, you pass a station
boarded with wood
shattered in forgotten wars.

Old men still stand
in dust by the tracks,
waving gnats away. You wave back

out of respect for something
dying, alone, in small towns.
At twilight, sun settles

low in your window
and, inside your car,
people return to local papers,

reading them back to front,
papers train-shaken and flapping
like the hands of those old men

by Manassas Station
who wait, continue to wait
for something to happen.

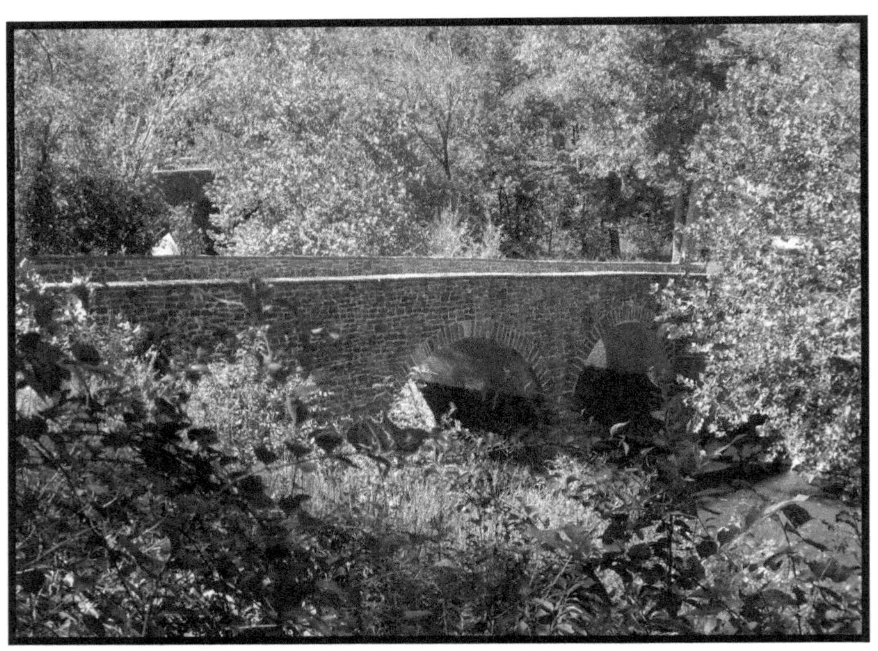

WILMER MCLEAN

Having experienced the war at first hand, McLean packed up his family and household goods and moved them far away seeking the quiet life of the planter. Imagine his surprise when, on April 9, 1865, he was approached by a group of Union and Confederate officers seeking a house with enough room in it to accommodate a joint conference. It was in his new home in Appomattox that General Lee and General Grant agreed to end the war.

V. C. Jones, First Manassas

July 20, 1861

Wilmer McLean leaned against
his splintered fence.
On the other side, war took shape
among trees and tall weeds.
He could feel the thunder
of movement at his feet,
the bump of wooden wheels
in his heart.

A farmer carries other weapons
to work clay into dust.
There have always been places
too hard for claws of steel.
Chunks of dirt could
fill a mortar and, exploded,
shatter bones twenty yards away.

Men in the woods knew:
seeds planted in the earth
toss their ragged heads to the air.
They knew blossoms of flesh
ready for harvest. These were
fields readied for planting,
suited to the kind of farming
a soldier might do.

July 21, 1861, early morning

McLean knew these empty hands
planting air in the earth.
In the morning, corn already waved
its hungry pattern. He held to this,
to the time it takes a farmer
to ready the land, plant and chop.

He arose before his wife,
leaving her on a pillow of dream.
Outside, tiny explosions of dust
burst beneath his steps.

His horse was damp to his touch
as he mounted to measure the distance
of his land, as if any man
owned what he stepped upon.

All night soldiers carried the warm
frost of steel, sparkling like streams
in moonlight. All morning
dust marked the road where they traveled.
Low explosions of sound McLean thought
he imagined, sounds so soft
maybe his wife and son had rolled over in bed.

McLean checked his fences, felt heat
hum through the wood, ran his thumb
along the splinters, snapping them loose
every few inches, pinching his hand
to remember how skin tears.
In the distance, sky rolled over
and he knew, only three miles away,
Stone Bridge had been mined.
He knelt and rubbed red earth
between the palms of his hands.

July 21, mid-morning

McLean held his son near him,
loaned him heat, more heat than a child
should know. McLean loaned his son
the callous of hands covering ears,
a winter's muffler that had pulled
corn from its stem, ripped it from
the cob, knew ripeness against a thumb.

His wife stood at the door,
her head bent as she listened
to Parrott rifles scream
through sunshine. She wiped
her forehead with her wrist.

McLean led his family to the barn.
A mile away, at Signal Hill,
Alexander scoured the horizon
until his binoculars stopped
in the fields beyond McLean's farm.

Morning sun glinted off brass rifles.
Bayonets and musket barrels
squinted at sun through the trees.
Alexander signaled,
twisting his body. McLean twisted

straw around his family,
surrounding them with beasts of labor.
Outside his door, soldiers collided,
close enough for McLean to see young men
wince from pain and sound,
the ax of war that separates
man from the land.

July 21, early afternoon

Where Bull Run touched his farm,
something passed between McLean
and his wife, something unseen but understood.
His son was the first
to find bodies slumped over the fence.

"This war," said McLean, "is no
tidy business." And he moved his
belongings farther west,
protesting this intrusion,
this sudden shift of death's
hot breath, this rifle of a life
he had pointed in one direction
and shot in another.

April 9, 1865, early morning, Appomattox

Politicians' tongues snap like whips
against horses. McLean knew
the sound, the brass shoulders
bouncing into his valley.

His hot face knew the odor
of death, the hollow eyes of the soldier
who has measured progress
in the thud of boot against body.

McLean knew beginning and end,
seed and harvest. He stirred the dust
with his shoes. Inside, his wife
readied to leave again,

this time loading her shoulders with the heavy ax
that severs war and the gentle threads
that cross in earthworm rugs
on the ground throughout the south.

ACKNOWLEDGEMENTS

Some of these poems have previously appeared in the following journals

New Laurel Review

Laurel Review

Tar River Poetry

Oxford Magazine

Four Quarters

Street Magazine

La Fusta

Hog River Review

Sou'wester

Appalachian Journal

Long Pond Review

The Dos Passos Review

Crop Dust

New York Quarterly

North Carolina Humanities Review

"Violence' appeared on The Poets Against the War website, *poetsagainstthewar.com,* 2002

"Building a House of History" first appeared in the anthology, *September 11, 2001: American Writers Respond.* Many thanks to Etruscan Press and editor, William Heyen.

"The Taste of Rope" and "Country Path" first appeared in a limited-edition chapbook, *The Taste of Rope,* Allegany Mountain Press, 1978. Many thanks to the editors.

"Manassas" won the *Four Quarters Poetry Prize.*

"Stillness" won The Madeline Sadin Award from *NYQ*.

"Tobacco Fields" first appeared in the anthology *Leaves of Greens.* Thanks to Alex Albright, editor.

"Swimming the Earth" first appeared in *Fear of the Coming Drought,* Mount Olive College Press, 2001. Thanks to Pepper Worthington.

Other poems in this collection appeared in chapbooks: *Poems of the Manassas Battlefield,* and *More Poems of the Manassas Battlefield,* Mount Olive College Press, 2016 and 2018

PHOTOGRAPHER BIO

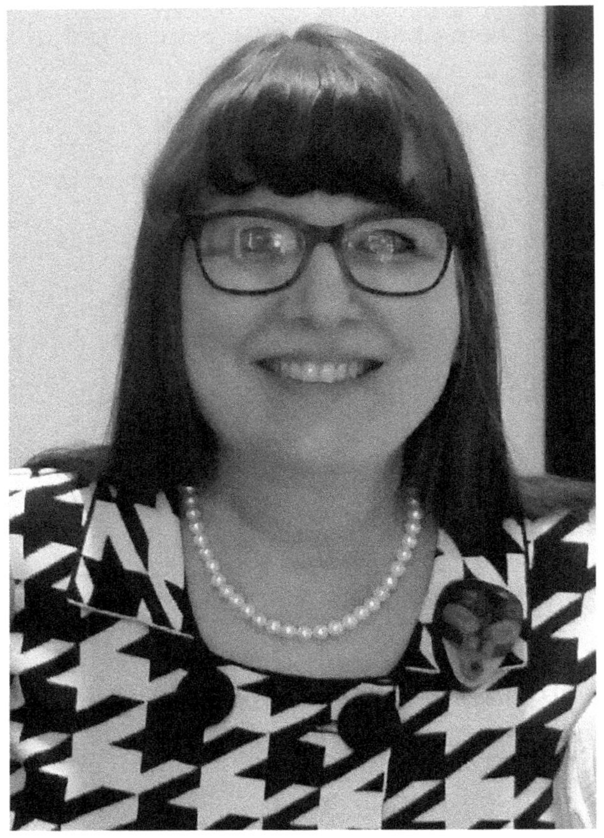

Of Cherokee and Meherrin descent, **Resa Crane Bizzaro** earned degrees in Creative Writing, Literature, and Composition and taught for more than thirty-five years. A recipient of a CCCC Scholars for the Dream Award, Resa served as a Co-Chair of the CCCC American Indian Caucus, a member of the CCCC Executive Committee, and a member or chair of many other professional committees. In 2012, Resa consulted at University of the Free State in South Africa in developing a literacy program. She has published articles on Native identity rhetorics, intergenerational Post-Traumatic Stress Disorder, contemporary poetry, and southern literature. Currently, Resa is an independent scholar and lives with her husband, Patrick, and son, Antonio, in western Pennsylvania. These photographs are Resa's first foray into collaborative publishing with her husband and his poetry.

AUTHOR BIO

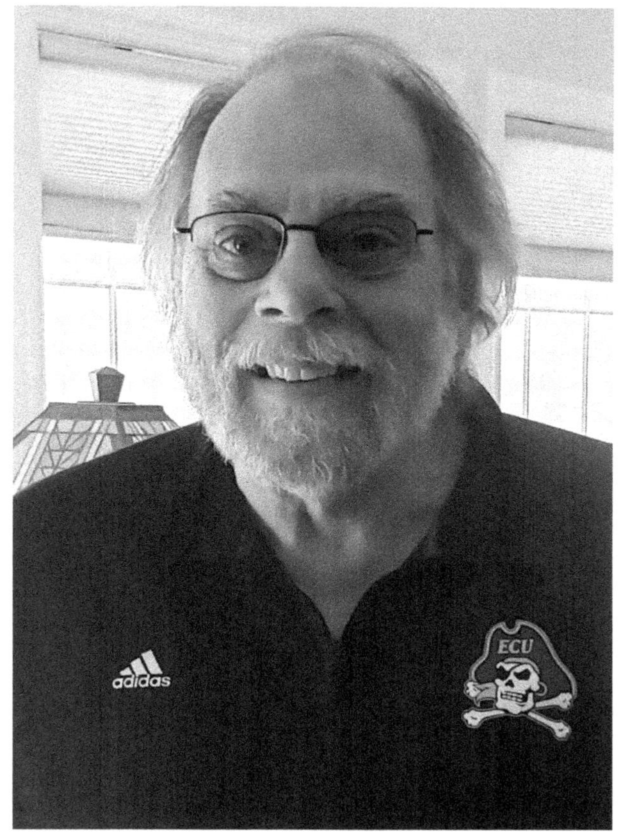

Patrick Bizzaro is the author of 12 poetry collections and chapbooks, two literary studies of Fred Chappell's work (LSU Press), a National Council of Teachers of English book on creative writing pedagogy, and many other publications. He traveled to South Africa in 2012 on a Fulbright grant to assist with an English language literacy program at University of the Free State. He is an award-winning teacher and Professor Emeritus of English at East Carolina University. He is a past winner of the Madeline Sadin Award from *New York Quarterly*.

www.ingramcontent.com/pod-product-compliance
Lightning Source LLC
LaVergne TN
LVHW010947110826
845149LV00015B/3245

* 9 7 8 1 9 5 9 3 4 6 0 1 2 *